Studies in Economic History

Aims and Scopes

This series from Springer provides a platform for works in economic history that truly integrate economics and history. Books on a wide range of related topics are welcomed and encouraged, including those in macro-economic history, financial history, labor history, industrial history, agricultural history, the history of institutions and organizations, spatial economic history, law and economic history, political economic history, historical demography, and environmental history.

Economic history studies have greatly developed over the past several decades through application of economics and econometrics. Particularly in recent years, a variety of new economic theories and sophisticated econometric techniques—including game theory, spatial economics, and generalized method of moment (GMM)—have been introduced for the great benefit of economic historians and the research community.

At the same time, a good economic history study should contribute more than just an application of economics and econometrics to past data. It raises novel research questions, proposes a new view of history, and/or provides rich documentation. This series is intended to integrate data analysis, close examination of archival works, and application of theoretical frameworks to offer new insights and even provide opportunities to rethink theories.

The purview of this new Springer series is truly global, encompassing all nations and areas of the world as well as all eras from ancient times to the present. The editorial board, who are internationally renowned leaders among economic historians, carefully evaluate and judge each manuscript, referring to reports from expert reviewers. The series publishes contributions by university professors and others well established in the academic community, as well as work deemed to be of equivalent merit.

More information about this series at http://www.springer.com/series/13279

Akira Hayami

Japan's Industrious Revolution

Economic and Social Transformations in the Early Modern Period

Springer

Akira Hayami
Fellow
The Japan Academy
Japan

Professor Emeritus
Keio University
Japan

ISSN 2364-1797 ISSN 2364-1800 (electronic)
Studies in Economic History
ISBN 978-4-431-55141-6 ISBN 978-4-431-55142-3 (eBook)
DOI 10.1007/978-4-431-55142-3

Library of Congress Control Number: 2015938586

Springer Tokyo Heidelberg New York Dordrecht London

Printed on acid-free paper

Springer Japan KK is part of Springer Science+Business Media (www.springer.com)

Preface to the English Edition

This book explains how economic and social transformations in pre-1600 Japan led to an industrious revolution in the early modern period, a profound change which made the vast majority of the population "industrious" – in a different sense from Professor Jan de Vries's thesis. While the de Vries thesis focuses on consumer behavior, the author argues that what happened in Japanese history was the rise of labor-intensive agriculture which was compatible with the rise of the market.

The volume is a modified version of *Kinsei nihon no keizai shakai* (Economic Society in Early Modern Japan), which was published by Reitaku University Press in 2004. Looking further back, it began with the 1973 edition of *Nihon ni okeru keizai shakai no tenkai* (Development of Economic Society in Japan), a textbook on the economic history of Japan written for undergraduates at Keio University. The state of research in economic history in 1970s Japan was still under the influence of Marxism which had dominated the 1950s and 1960s, yet economic growth due to "Japanese-style capitalism" had begun. Confronting the reality that economic standards that departed from those of the low ones of the immediate postwar days were starting, studies of economic history from new angles grounded in economic development theory and quantitative observations – not those of traditional descriptivist methods – became prominent. Yet, none of these methods satisfied the masses, so textbooks aimed at undergraduates written from a variety of standpoints also lined the shelves at bookstores, and beginners could not figure out which one to choose.

Such being the case, the aforementioned textbook is a compilation of the author's historical perspective. Up until that point, the author had limited himself to three research areas: studies on rural villages in the Kantō district (where the observational results primarily taught the author about the creation of market economies in that areas), studies on the cadastral surveys performed at the beginning of the early modern period, and demographic analysis of rural villages from the latter half of the seventeenth century until the Meiji Restoration (1868). On these three bases, the author published a 128-page textbook in 1973.

Naturally, although it was an "economic history of Japan," the ancient and medieval periods (prior to the latter half of the sixteenth century) are covered only briefly, and the author does not specifically elaborate on the Meiji Restoration onward. It goes without saying that it does not incorporate trends in recent research in economic history (global economic history, comparative economic history).

However, looking back on this volume, the author saw that a hypothesis had started to form in the author's mind as to the course where economic modernization was achieved through a market economy: the ancient state system which was highly centralized; economic as well as religious authority was actually the factor which did not permit the development of market economy; and what enabled it was a society where religious and secular authority, in addition to political power and economic agents, were separated. This was greatly influenced by the author's experiences during stopovers – albeit short – in the Middle and Near East, South Asia, and Southeast Asia on the author's way to and from the author's studies abroad in 1963 and 1964.

For example, the colossal sense the author felt when the author ascended the pyramids in Egypt: the massive amount of labor required to construct these royal tombs, colossal structures irrelevant to everyday lives in an era where the only tools were rollers. Thinking about the pyramids and comparing them to the modern Egyptian homes spread out below, the author noticed this major gap and questioned himself as to its causes. In the end, the answer the author discovered was that this disparity was due to the nature of the ruling class (ruling elites) and the common people at the bottom.

In ancient societies, there was no middle class between the ruling and ruled classes, and the ruling class was almighty in monopolizing politics and economics, as well as culture and religion. Viewed in this light, the ruled classes were almost animals in human form, and if they were worked to death, all that was needed was to start a war and bring back prisoners. Therefore, it was not at all difficult to build these massive structures that modern people find incomprehensible. The scale of the massive burial mounds in fourth to sixth century Japan is also on a par with the structures built elsewhere in the ancient world. In short, an ancient society also existed, if not a grand scale, in Japan.

What dismantled these ancient societies – including Japan's – was the encounter with religion (not folk beliefs, but ones where gods and scriptures exist). Religion possesses transcendental absolutes, so once religion enters ancient society, its secular ruling class is no longer almighty. In addition, with the appearance of missionaries who transmit the scriptures to believers and intermediaries who spread the teachings among the masses, the rulers distinguished them from the ordinary masses and granted them a protected status, giving birth to a middle class. Political rulers embracing a particular religion meant they would lose their prior almighty authority, but the key to dismantling ancient society can be found in their unawareness of this paradox.

Another factor is commerce. Commerce is said to be "as old as the history of mankind," but in ancient societies, it was difficult for the masses to engage in commerce peacefully. All profits went to the ruling class, and circumstances were such that commoners were not permitted to obtain profits through commerce. However, once the separation of religious and secular authority began and secular rulers were no longer absolute, commercial activity by the masses appeared.

What first started as barter developed into markets – particularly regular markets – and transactional distances shifted from near-distance to long-distance. Products also did not incur shipping charges at first, and items with significant value differences – such as jewelry and precious metals – were traded, and these came to be exchanged in the form of gifts and reciprocity.

Currency was born as a result of expanded commercial activity, and this currency stimulated it, acting as a positive feedback function. However, currency did not always stimulate the economy in that manner. In Japan, copper coins were minted in 708, an imitation of those minted in Tang dynasty China, but since the economy was not sufficiently developed to require currency, its circulation was also limited, and minting ceased 250 years later. We might call it "currency before its time."

The conversion of *shōen nengu* payments into currency began during the twelfth and thirteenth centuries, and large quantities of Sung and Ming dynasty coins were imported throughout the fourteenth and fifteenth centuries. The economy came to require currency. The chaos of the Sengoku (Warring States Period) passed, and the Tokugawa shogunate established the currency system that the short-lived regimes of Oda Nobunaga and Toyotomi Hideyoshi could not. This system, with gold and silver as standard and copper coins as supplemental currency, was not a simple one: exchange rates between gold and silver were introduced, and in several domains, *hansatsu*, a domainal paper currency, was issued. In any case, by the Edo Period everyone residing in Japan knew of currency and came to use it.

From this, Japan finally became a currency-based economy, and with that came developments in a variety of systems, facilities, and professions, in addition to learning and thought. The author calls this condition "economic society." Naturally, economic society was not made up in a day. However, between the period prior to the emergence of economic society and the one that followed, there were major changes in the lifestyle, thinking, and values of those who lived there. Referring to the period following the emergence of economic society as "modern" is acceptable, but this volume will call this era "early modern" and examine how it developed.

A great deal of knowledge and works have been useful for the author to establish the idea of the history of Japan developed in this volume. Here the author wishes to point out just five works that decisively impacted on the author's idea to write this volume: (1) John Hicks, *A Theory of Economic History* (Oxford University Press, 1969); (2) Henri Pirenne, *Mohammed and Charlemagne* (Allen and Unwin, 1939); (3) B. H. Slicher van Bath, *The Agrarian History of Western Europe*, A.D. 500–1850 (Edward Arnold, 1966); (4) Robert Heilbroner, *The Making of Economic Society* (Prentice-Hall, 1963); and (5) Douglass C. North and Robert Paul Thomas, *The Rise of the Western World* (Cambridge University Press, 1973).

Finally, the author wishes to deeply thank Osamu Saito, a former student of the author and Professor Emeritus of Hitotsubashi University, who read and checked the manuscripts of several chapters of this book at the final stage of the editing process. Without Osamu's help, I couldn't have completed this book.

Tokyo, Japan Akira Hayami

Contents

About the Author

Akira Hayami is a member of the Japan Academy and a correspondent member of the Academy of the Moral and Political Sciences, France. He is professor emeritus of Keio University (Tokyo), the International Research Center for Japanese Studies (Kyoto), and Reitaku University (Kashiwa). Hayami is also the former vice president of the International Association of Economic History, honorary president of the International Committee of Historical Demography and former president of the Socio-economic History Society in Japan. He was awarded the Order of Cultural Merit (Japan) in 2009.

Major publications include *The Historical Demography of Pre-Modern Japan* (University of Tokyo Press, 2001), *Population, Family and Society in Pre-Modern Japan* (Global Oriental, 2009), and *Population and Family in Early-Modern Central Japan* (International Research Center for Japanese Studies, 2010). He also co-edited with Ad Van der Woude and Jan de Vries the volume *Urbanization in History: A Process of Dynamic Interactions* (Oxford University Press, 1990) and co-edited with Osamu Saito and Ronald P. Toby the book *Emergence of Economic Society in Japan, 1600–1859* (Oxford University Press, 2004).

Hayami's major contributions include the application of historical demography methods to early-modern Japanese data, the finding of fresh facts made possible by the methodological breakthrough, which in turn emancipated early-modern Japanese historiography from a "dark age" imagery, and the coining of the term "Industrious Revolution."

Glossary

bakufu-han (bakuhan) system	Political system consisting of bakufu and han (daimyō domains)
gōshi	Landed samurai
kemi	Field inspection
kokuga	Provincial headquarters
komononari	Miscellaneous taxes
konden	Reclaimed rice fields
kuge	Court aristocracy. A term referring to the emperor and court aristocrats
kumigashira	Head of the goningumi
kuraichi	Land under shogun's or daimyō's direct rule
nago	Hereditary servant
nakama	Guild
nanushi	Village headman
rakuichi rakuza	Free markets, open guilds
shōya	Village headman
shugo	Military provincial governor
tato	Land manager
tenryō	Shogunal lands
yui	Cooperative work group in rice planting
yusoden	Taxable fields
za	A trade or craft guild that originated in the eleventh century. Most active in the Muromachi Period

List of Figures and Tables

Provinces in Mid-Edo Period

51. Aki
8. Awa (1)
56. Awa (2)
37. Awaji
50. Bingo
49. Bitchū
48. Bizen
59. Bungo
58. Buzen
61. Chikugo
60. Chikuzen
2. Dewa
12. Echigo
16. Echizen
13. Etchu
46. Harima
20. Hida
63. Higo
5. Hitachi
62. Hizen
42. Hōki
64. Hyūga
29. Iga
41. Inaba
27. Ise
45. Iwami
55. Iyo
21. Izu
35. Izumi
44. Izumo
15. Kaga
18. Kai
34. Kawachi
7. Kazusa
36. Kii
3. Kōzuke
24. Mikawa
47. Mimasaka
26. Mino
9. Musashi
1. Mutsu
53. Nagato
14. Noto
43. Oki
30. Ōmi
65. Ōsumi
25. Owari
11. Sado
10. Sagami
54. Sanuki
66. Satsuma
33. Settsu
28. Shima
6. Shimōsa
4. Shimotsuke
19. Shinano
52. Suō
22. Suruga
40. Tajima
38. Tanba
39. Tango
57. Tosa
23. Tōtōmi
17. Wakasa
31. Yamashiro
32. Yamato

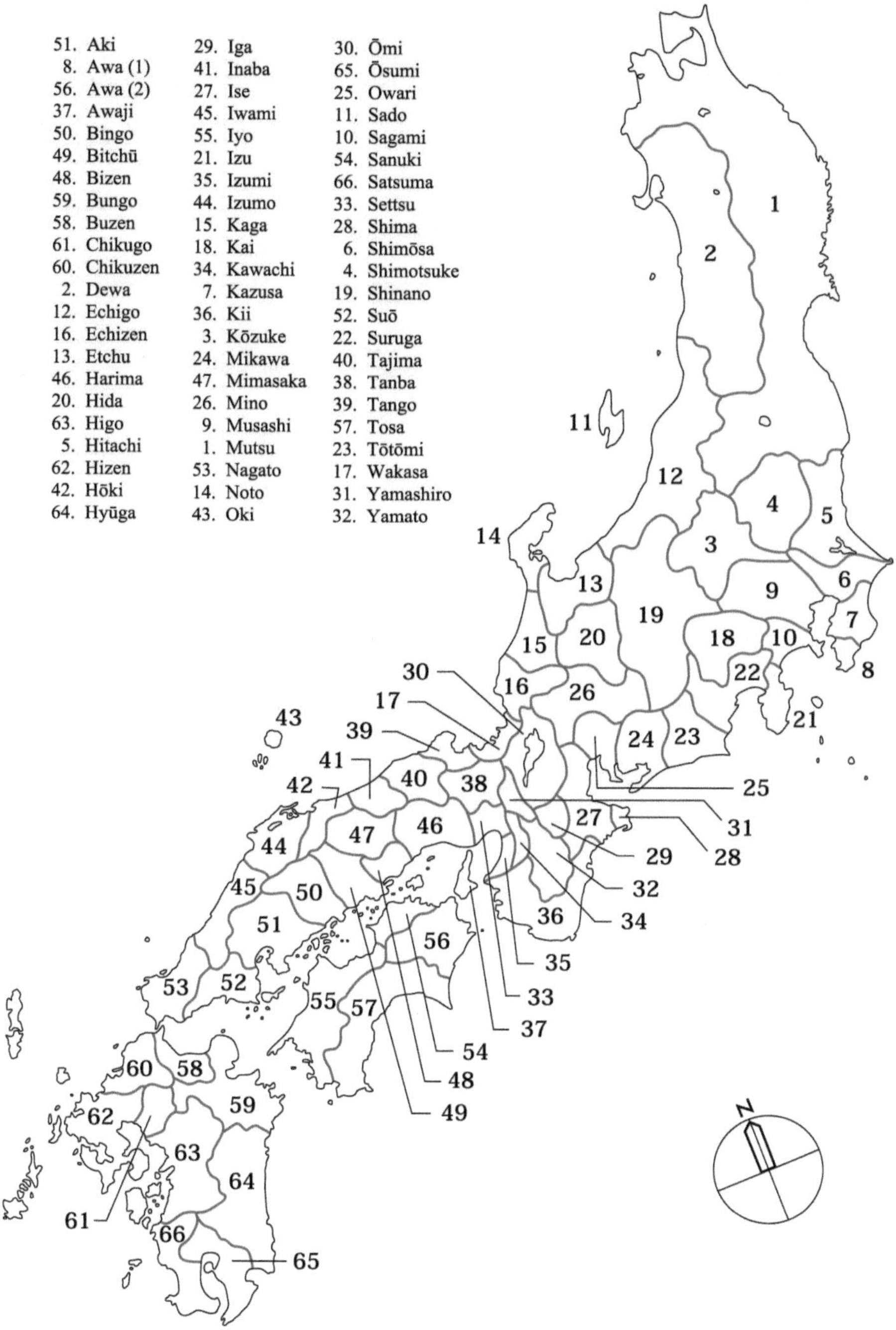

Chapter 1
Introduction: Viewpoints and Methods in the Economic History of Japan

1.1 Scope and Methods of Economic History

Taken literally, economic history is an academic discipline whose purpose is to seek out the developmental processes of economic phenomena occurring in everyday life within the bounds of history. Therefore, as a field, it can be said to reside in an intermediate area between economics and history. There is not much constructive meaning in stating which field a certain discipline belongs to, since fixating on such things leaves little prospect for disciplinary synthesis or new developments. However, in comparison to cases where its content is clearly based on expressions such as "theory" or "history" within economics, when it is evident that it is in an intermediate area from the onset, its character as a discipline is no longer simple. The methods of economic history clearly have economic and historical approaches; furthermore, these contain the differences in their worldview, historical view, and adopted methodology, and so on. Consequently, even works that equally claim to be "economic history" have an extremely broad range of methods and viewpoints. In the past as well, people who were called economic historians were in some cases economists and in some cases were scholars listed amongst the names of historians. In addition, it is by no means easy to distinguish "economy" from other social phenomena, as well as psychological factors, and in some cases, the very act of handling them separately is a mistake.

This is more or less the case even to this day, but it was all the more so the further back one ventured into the past. It stands to reason that there will be differences in the content and methods between "economic history" in an era where political,

---

For many expressions on the events and institutions of Japanese history, this work is indebted to the most authentic work, *The Cambridge History of Japan*, 6 volumes, particularly to volumes 2–5, i.e. Shively and McCullough (1999), Yamamura (1990), Hall and McClain (1991), and Jansen (1989). Also an additional debt is owed to the first volume of *The Economic History of Japan: 1600–1990*, i.e. Hayami, Saito and Toby (1999).

A. Hayami, *Japan's Industrious Revolution*, Studies in Economic History,
DOI 10.1007/978-4-431-55142-3_1

social, and religious phenomena each merged with economic phenomena, and where fixed economic principles did not exist independently, and "economic history" in an era where economic principles themselves have made significant advances in their own right. Even today, conditions where market mechanisms are a "site" for economics are one model, and in reality, it is clear that other non-market elements have been woven into economics. Also, compared to societies where methods selected by political leaders comprise the content of the "economics," the manner in which economics and people relate to each other will differ greatly. In the latter case, politics and economics are in an inseparable relationship.

Demarcating the area of economic history in this manner is difficult, not to mention the impossibility of seeking out some kind of methodological unity. However, economic history is capable of incorporating the very diversity and complexity surveyed above into the object of analysis as a historical product, and more to the point, they must also be made into objects of analysis.

From this vantage point, in dealing with the "economic history of Japan" here, it is necessary to clearly indicate the angle from which he views economic history. Naturally, what is presented here is just one possibility. The intent is not to say "Believe this!"; rather, it is to thrust what is written here against the viewpoint held by the reader, or the viewpoint that the reader is in the process of holding, and create a relationship of tension. Thus, the intention is for the reader to understand that it is precisely within this kind of relationship of tension where the opportunity for creative academic development exists.

1.2 The Object of this Volume

The object of an economic history of Japan is the examination of issues such as the causes, courses, results, and impacts of economic phenomena which occur within the object limited by the geography of Japan. However, phenomena outside of Japan are brought into view as long as they are relevant to Japan, or if a comparison with external phenomena creates a better or more precise understanding of economic phenomena in Japan. Also, as stated earlier, there are many cases where economic phenomena cannot be separated from social relationships outside of economics. In these cases, it is natural that an analysis will inevitably enter non-economic fields.

However, these circumstances do not mean that the scope of analysis may be broadened without limit. Here, in writing this volume there is an attempt to set the following limits. First, this work will provide an overview of the developmental process of history in Japan and establish a period when economic principles became independent from other social phenomena and commenced a self-revolution – this will be called "the establishment of economic society," which will be explained later. This period will serve as a boundary line to provide a general division to what came before and after it. For the period prior to the establishment of economic society, emphasis will be placed instead on the elucidation of the conditions that define economics in its periphery, in other words, the conditions other than economics, from the standpoint of economics within social phenomena. In the period after the establishment of economic society, it becomes a narrative held tightly together by economics, but it conforms to the changes in society itself. What is also important is an examination of the period and method of social change in this sense, and a chapter has been devoted to it. Also, some people may find it odd that the scope of this study largely ends at the end of the Edo Period and the beginning of the Meiji Restoration (1868). For one thing, the scope covered as economic history certainly can include the modern period, but thoughts on this, which will be explained below, are that in a variety of ways what characterizes industrialization in Japan is almost all historical experiences prior to the Restoration, and there is nothing outside of "economic history" that can deal with this period. Another point is that it was determined that in light of issues such as quantity, content, and methodology, it would be appropriate to cover the new era as "economic history in early-modern Japan" in an independent volume.

1.3 The Modern Era as an Analytical Point of Departure

The world we now live in is experiencing the greatest amount of change since the dawn of humanity. One aspect of this is that economy is also in a state of extreme qualitative and quantitative flux. These changes are commonly called modernization or industrialization, or even computerization. What is also important is that this industrialization is also diverse in its degree and methods. Generally, countries with advanced industrialization are called "developed countries," and those that lag behind are called "developing countries," but as general labels each of these categories is in accordance with rough geographical position, and the former is associated with the "north" and the latter the "south." The north–south issue is one created from the disparities between the two. On the other hand, two different methods can be seen in the achievement of industrialization as well. Specifically, one is via price mechanisms (in other words, the method where economic development is achieved with competition in markets between economic agents as a condition) and the other is the method where industrialization is realized via government policy based on plans formulated by political leaders. Until very recently, capitalism and socialism were the systems representing these two methods, but by no means do they provide an adequate nomenclature. In common parlance, the former was called the "western" group and the latter the "eastern" group. Furthermore, these were linked to political systems and ideology and the world was divided by the so-called Iron Curtain, creating this east–west problem until very recent years.

Theoretically, combinations of east and west, and north and south, would result in the existence of four types, but as a practical matter, these four types are by no means simple, and the combinations become even more complicated, and to a certain degree, fluid. Even looking at the degree of development, there is no clear line separating the developed countries from the developing countries; they form a continuum. One idea is to create the category of "semi-developed country." Also, it would be one thing if economic development were limited to quantitative measurable aspects, but when cases of non-measurable aspects, or non-economic fields, are put into view, it becomes clear that it would be no easy matter for the standard of "developed countries" to create this category. For example, a situation is possible where one country is a developed country economically, but is politically and socially behind, or another country is a developed country insofar as the production aspects of its economy, but is conspicuously behind in its expansion of social fundamentals. Even if limited to cases that can be quantitatively measured, many economic indices are volatile, and countries can rise to the level of a developed country in the short term, or conversely, stagnate for a long time – essentially, the problem is that distribution is along a continuum, and "volatile" is the only way to describe this situation.

The same holds true for the other methodology, and do countries which economically engage in completely free competition exist today? Also, in a word, we say "capitalism" and "socialism,"; but even if principles exist as principles realistically, there are various mutations, and in some cases, it even appears mixed. Depending on the country, there are also non-socialist planned economies, or socialist named capitalist countries.

1.4 Typology of Industrialization

However, when an attempt at classification is made keeping this kind of complexity sufficiently in mind, in cases where this industrialization is grounded in the field of economics, generally speaking the following can be said.

From the outward phenomenological aspects, one group consists of countries that commenced industrialization prior to the end of the nineteenth century and adopted so-called capitalism as its method, in other words, countries such as those in Western Europe, North America, and Australia and Japan. The members of this group are advanced industrial nations, and politically, have adopted parliamentary democracy. The other group includes all other countries, specifically, those whose industrialization commenced during the twentieth century and have adopted non-capitalist methods (socialism being one of these) as their means of development. However, these groupings are ultimately cases that treat the attainment of industrialization after the fact, and the premise is that this will happen when we place the performer of modernization, particularly the internal elements of subject formation, outside of our consideration. This is why from the standpoint of the performer of modernization, or when arguments are made placing spiritual and internal elements on an axis, groupings of entirely different content become possible.

Fig. 1.1 Typology of Industrialization

Type	Agent	Condition
I	+	+
II	−	+
III	+	−
IV	−	−

1.5 Agents and Conditions of Industrialization

In the development of history, however, when considering a particular change, an analysis of the agent that promotes its change is necessary, but at the same time, an analysis of the conditions that accept this change and propel the agent – whatever the motive may be – is required. Even in the change known as industrialization, by assigning "plus" and "minus" symbols to the existence and absence to the elements of "agent" and "condition," four combinations are formed, as seen in Fig. 1.1.

The four combinations in Fig. 1.1 can be explained as follows. When "agent" and "condition" are both positive, industrialization commences the quickest in this type of society and will be achieved with greater ease. In Type II, where there is no agent but the conditions are prepared, independent industrialization does not occur, but industrialization would likely begin to progress if there is an external influence. Type III appears in a state where only the agent is formed, and industrialization will likely take a different course from Types I and II. For Type IV, it is natural that as is, industrialization cannot take place. As an aside, when considering the aforementioned model, agents and conditions are strictly delineated. However, in actuality, they cannot be said to exist independently. Formation of an agent class is a product of conditions up to a certain degree. At least their spontaneous formation cannot be seen in areas with no conditions. It is in that sense that Type III is interpreted as unrealistic. However, due to interference between types, there may be cases where agents oriented toward modernization are formed in areas where conditions are not present. Moreover, whether it is a country or a society, it does not mean that it will remain as one of these types for an eternity. History is precisely changes such as the formation proceeding in places where there was no agent and conditions starting to align in places where there were none.

1.6 Agents and the so-called Bourgeois Revolution

Incidentally, what specifically would the agents of industrialization and conditions be like? The agents, in this case, are a group of people with an inclination toward industrialization, be it conscious or unconscious. Entrepreneurs, management, government, political leaders, and others make up the primary members, but broadly interpreted, intellectuals as opinion leaders, laborers, and producers such as farmers or the leaders of consumer organizations can be included. Also, it is not absolutely necessary for them to be individuals – they may be organizations as well. The formation of agents occurs when these people and organizations start to observe universal values in industrialization. Therefore, first it is necessary that the conditions toward industrialization be arranged in their periphery, or that within cognizable limits these conditions exist. Next, it is desirable that the forces that impede the promotion of industrialization be removed. In this sense, a bourgeois revolution is the removal of obstacles. However, a word of caution: bourgeois revolutions are by no means completely carried out in all areas; rather, it is a continuum from its onset and is still in progress. The larger and more entrenched the obstacle, the greater the intensity of the bourgeois revolution; conversely, if these obstacles are not so stubborn, situations occur where the bourgeois revolution follows a relatively peaceful course as a phenomenon. The matter of the "completeness" and "incompleteness" of revolutions is a separate issue.

1.7 On Conditions

1.7.1 Conditions of Industrialization

Next, we will consider conditions. In other words, the "conditions of industrialization" means the existence of a society where economic rationality can be easily realized. Humans are often said to possess multi-dimensional values. Various values – political, religious, social, economic, and conventional – regulate people's thoughts and actions. Among these values, economic values sever their subordinate relationships to others and become independent, and what gradually dominates is a current that exists as an undercurrent toward industrialization. In past eras, economic values were subordinated to morality, religion, and politics. In such a society, it was conspicuously difficult for people to behave economically. Taking medieval Europe as an example, the prohibition on usury was required by Church doctrine, and peasants had various restrictions imposed on their economic activities, as they had no social and geographical mobility. Under these circumstances, the degree to which their economic activities realized economic rationality was extremely low.

1.7.2 Conditions where Economic Principles are Nonexistent

As a model, we will consider a society where economic rationality has not been realized, and consequently, economic principles do not clearly exist. In an extreme case, a state where economic principles are nonexistent is one where, for instance, prices do not exist for products, workers are employed at any wage, and interest rates on capital are not fixed. Under such circumstances, demand and supply curves for labor and capital, or assets, cannot be drawn. However, in reality, this kind of situation is not possible. Laborers living solely on wages cannot live on wages below the subsistence level. There are unlikely to be merchants, other than charitable organizations, who willingly sell below cost. However, on the other hand, much like the society where economic principles clearly exist, it must be acknowledged that a state where people are economically sensitive is a special type of society.

1.8 Economic Society

This change can be expressed with the phrase "the sudden rise of markets" (Hicks 1969; see also van Bath 1963). How many markets are there as sites for economic activity in the society in which we now live? All capital, products, and labor flow through "markets," where "prices" are formed, and adjustments in supply and demand are performed. Whether they like it or not, people must conduct their economic activity here. People act to gain maximum utility and profit with the least cost and sacrifice. Therefore, information must be easily attainable, and economic choices must be made freely.

We will call a society an "economic society" when its people act as such. Naturally, the transition from a pre-economic society to an economic society is made in stages, and since this does not apply to all aspects of human life, this creates problems in how to measure the formation of economic society. However, this very fact is the determining "condition" for capitalistic industrialization. If these conditions are present, it is possible to pull the capital, labor, and technology required for industrialization from all parts of society. In areas that do not have these kinds of conditions, for example, wealth that exists in a corner of society is nothing more than an expression of the power of the strata of society possessing this wealth. Excess labor is merely accumulated without making any kind of contribution to economic development.

Therefore, when and how the formation of this type of economic society occurs is an extremely large element in determining that country's type of industrialization. For instance, the following can be said. In cases where subjects are formed prior to the formation of conditions, and when industrialization is achieved, all of the resources required for industrialization are not fulfilled via markets, at least for the time being, so some kind of forced measures become necessary to attain them. Viewed from an economic perspective, socialism is without parallel as this type of measure. As a consequence, socialist economy is one of the industrialization methods chosen in Type III societies.

When "conditions" (which equals the formation of economic society) greatly precedes demand for industrialization, this means that the individual conditions leading to industrialization exist within the people's everyday lives, since economic activity is already under way in the market. At most, what was required for industrialization was just the organization and acceleration of these factors and greater efficiency in accumulating the required resources.

Of course, in these cases as well, there are likely to be differences depending on whether performer formation was present at the same time. However, at any rate, industrialization without performers is inconceivable. Sooner or later, or whether they are sufficient or insufficient, there must be subjects to promote industrialization, and once these are formed the process of industrialization will likely converge into a similar type. However, when there is rapid performer formation, since this is mainly carried out in accordance with demands for industrialization, it is conceivable that it will be out of sync with the other aspects of modernization, in other words, its cultural and social aspects. Ultimately, performer formation itself is a product of history, and over the long term, in cases where it forms spontaneously, modernization is likely to proceed in a balanced manner while maintaining its relationships to that society's non-economic aspects.

1.9 Paths to Industrialization

When the types of industrialization are expressed graphically taking the aforementioned discussion into consideration, the results are as follows:

(A) Type IV → Type II → Type I
(B) Type IV → Type III → (Type I)

However, within Sequence (A), there are differences in the length of time Type II was experienced, and it is difficult to say that Type I in Sequence (B) has already been achieved, so judgment has to be withheld as to whether it is attainable. In Sequence (A), this includes England, where bourgeois revolutions already commenced in the seventeenth century and the Industrial Revolution in the eighteenth century, followed by the major continental powers in Western Europe and North America, and so on. Also, this applies to former British colonies such as Australia. Japan is distinctive in having experienced the longest Type II, but in the end, it can be included in this category. The long-established framework of economic history research in Japan primarily considers this category to be the only possible method for industrialization and positioned Japan within it. This method used England, which experienced a relatively short Type II, as a mirror and measured Japan's distance from it. This can be said to be linked to the practical matter of Japan's attempts to rush into industrialization under slogans such as "Catch Up and Overtake the Developed Western Countries."

Sequence (B) can cover countries such as the former Soviet Union, China, India, Asian, and African nations, and the nations of Central and South America. In these regions, "conditions" are in an immature state, or in extreme cases, nonexistent, and were forcibly industrialized due to the impact of the industrialization of the Western countries, and had to seek out a way to deal with this. As a solution, so-called socialist economics was adopted in some of these countries, separate from political ideology (of course, in many cases they overlap). However, truly this system was far too short in time and experience to render a judgment as to whether it could bring about a Type I society. In this regard, in particular, the introduction of so-called profit motives in the production of food and consumer products in the socialist sphere, which began in 1989 with the collapse of the economy of the former Soviet Union, is a noteworthy phenomenon.

1.10 Two Paths to Development in Economic History

A more detailed analysis of these two categories is shown in Fig. 1.2. In Fig. 1.2, Sequence (A) experiences a "decentralized society," which internally brings forth elements (the largest would be the ability to create an economic society that can realize economic rationality) that negate the "decentralized society" itself, and demonstrates the development from Type II to Type I. Sequence (B) experienced "civilization" in some areas which developed under a Type IV society, known as an "ancient society," but they did not have the ability to negate it and advance to the next stage, resulting in its "fossilization." Also, in a number of areas – as far as we know – this course elapsed unable to possess a value system, civilization, or nation as a single, unified entity. Also, the economic, technological, and military disparities created in the process of attaining industrialization in Sequence (A) shocked the entire world like a burst dam upon entering the nineteenth century, and colonization progressed. Finally, during the twentieth century (in particular, the latter half) there was opposition to this condition, and modernization deeply colored by nationalism commenced in Sequence (B).

Incidentally, even in Sequence (A), the process of a decentralized society forming required an impact from Sequence (B). A society vaguely categorized as "undeveloped" starts to move as a society by incorporating a variety of cultural elements developed under colossal ancient civilizations – the three key major elements being universal religion, literacy, and nation-building ability – while using them for sustenance. Also, it ultimately arrived at a decentralized society characterized by a separation

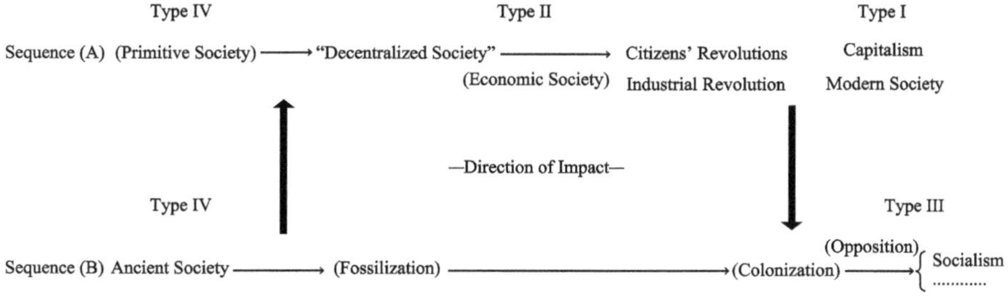

Fig. 1.2 Two Paths to Development in Economic History

of religion and politics and a separation of political and economic matters. When we try to look at the formation of Western European feudalistic society, historical chance encounters such as contact with Rome and the infiltration of Christianity were required conditions.

If these circumstances are examined even a little, changes in each category never form independently within the category; rather, it is evident that the mutual relationship between categories plays an extremely great role. We can say that here is where the term "world history" has meaning.

1.11 "Decentralized Society"

However, as demonstrated in Fig. 1.2 there is only one major exception – the shift from "decentralized society" to modern society. Here, there are no traces of any influence from the other categories. They are changes that occurred within the category. Therefore, regarding these parts, the development of history was formulaic and inevitable. Based on the fact that modern Western European society directly came into being in this manner, it is not strange that the historical view created there was strongly influenced by the inevitable historical changes actually taking place before their very eyes. This kind of thinking is a theory of evolution applied to history.

However, when an attempt is made to explain all aspects of history with this kind of thinking, one suddenly runs into a wall. There is not a single case where the transition from a so-called ancient society to a decentralized one, or from a developed capitalist society to a socialist one, was inevitably carried out internally. Speaking for the latter, socialism was instead seen in places where the realistic development of a capitalist economy was not possible.

1.12 Historical Approach

As a framework for thinking about history, if it were possible for the approach where the two categories shown here and their interrelationships, or the combination of their internal developments, to explain, without contradiction, the historical truths that we all know today – of course, there are several exceptions to this, there are intermediate states, and it is necessary to set limits – however, there is no reason to be bound by existing old historical views. Rather, the framework presented here should be aggressively squared against historical facts, and exposed to the trials of verification.

Now, when using the framework presented earlier, there are several matters that require caution. Here, the two categories are presented contrastively, but since these have both been abstracted, as a practical matter, there are several intermediate models and temporary variations. Imitation and mobility are two of the abilities possessed by humans. There are countless examples of a system being introduced, or a system being forced upon people by powerful political leaders. Rather, in reality, it may be more accurate to say that the social conditions of these countries are lined up in a continuum between these two categories. However, regardless of these, it is possible to provide examples of the most typical models and specific historical experiences in their respective aspects.

For example, in the area of modern social formation in Sequence (A), there likely would not be much room for disagreement if England were presented as an example. Sequence (B) could be represented by China in the area of modernization. However, on the other hand, when looking at Japan, it would be possible to consider Japan's modernization during the Meiji Period to contain the elements of Sequence (B) to a considerable degree, considering the role of government in the time. Therefore, it is not the case that the two categories exist as extremely rigid entities, and that all the nations of the world are arranged so that they clearly belong to one category or the other. Also, realistically, the matter of which category a particular country belongs to does not depend solely on that country's domestic circumstances. For example, even today, there are numerous cases where the particulars of a so-called system are determined to a considerable degree by international politics and military relationships. A root cause of the conflict after World War II was a "compulsion" that was largely created by these types of circumstances. It is precisely for this reason that the "fall of the Berlin Wall" in 1989 released the Eastern and Central European countries incorporated in the former Soviet sphere of influence up to that point to Western Europe.

Our presentation of this framework here is ultimately from an internal interpretation within the development of history. Even assuming that a situation where a single country cannot exist ignoring international relations is a historical product, as in the modern world, it is not the case that all of these matters were decided inside of history.

As an ultimate limit, the problem remains as to what social unit is used in this framework. If we are speaking of the present, the nation is this unit, and the economy can also be understood as a single, national unit, much like national income. However, this was not necessarily true in the past. Prior to the creation of the modern nation–state, one should look at Germany and Italy prior to the nineteenth century for examples of how the concept of "country" was not always clear. Going even further back, one may question whether "countries" existed in Europe prior to ethnic migrations and the creation of tribal states, or the Japanese archipelago prior to the Asuka Period. In that case, we could use tribes or regions as a unit, but tribes move and become mixed. Either approach has its strengths and weaknesses. The formation of the nation and its people is itself built in to the development of history.

1.13 Key Points and Summary

Several key points can be pointed out when reexamining this framework after establishing these various limits. The experience of "decentralized society" in the course for Sequence (A) is extremely important, viewed from that society's later development. Moreover, for the formation of "decentralized society" itself, outside influences are decisive. Next, why does this decentralized society dismantle itself, how are the elements that bring about internal collapse – the creation of economic society – built up, and how did dismantling progress? These problems serve as a support when examining prior eras where fully-fledged industrialization has commenced from the standpoint of economic history. This volume will deal with Japanese history from the same vantage point.

1.14 Periodization in Economic History

This introduction will conclude with a discussion of periodization in history, particularly economic history. For the names of historical eras, there are cases where they serve to divide eras, and there are cases where they are names given out of convenience. European historical divisions, such as ancient, medieval, and modern have a strong tendency to serve the former function, whereas Japanese divisions, such as the Kamakura Period and Muromachi Period, are examples of divisions which have a strong tendency to serve the latter function, making them epochs marking changes in political authority. Periodization in economic history is a quite difficult matter. Economic change differs from political and systemic change, and in many cases, it is gradual and accompanied by regional differences. Economic change does not necessarily correspond with political revolutions, except for the modernization in the societies in Sequence (B). By no means did the Meiji Restoration mean the immediate formation of a capitalist economic society. Even with an approach where divisions such as slave system, serf system and capitalist system are made based on a society's basic production structure, an understanding of transition periods is accompanied by great difficulty. What has been adopted in the economic history of Japan thus far has been in accordance with old-fashioned developmental stage theory – a hunter economy, an agrarian economy, a commercial economy, an industrial economy, and a credit economy, or the application of Marxist views of history, or borrowing categories from political history or general history. More thought should be given to fixed categories in economic history. For example, regarding Western European agricultural history, a recent work divided it into two periods: a period where agricultural products were directly consumed, and a period where agricultural products were indirectly consumed, with the year 1150 as the boundary (van Bath 1963). These categories are suited to agricultural history, and attention has been paid to its complete independence from those of general history, such as medieval and modern. These types of attempts should be made more often in Japan as well. This volume uses conventional Japanese historical divisions such as ancient, medieval, and early modern, and political history divisions such as Nara Period, Heian Period, or Kamakura Period simply as names (just like saying "such-and-such century"), and not as names with significance in economic history. In contrast, the periodization used here was established from the viewpoint of the formation of economic society. In particular, the period after the formation of economic society is divided into two periods: before and after industrialization was fully under way (with the 1890s as the boundary), but this volume is concerned with the period before that.

1.15 Summary of the Introduction

The introduction has presented a viewpoint that asks why Japan's industrialization was attained through capitalist means. The reason is that capitalist economics is neither the sole means that enables industrialization, nor is it a stage that every country or every ethnic group is required to experience.

The creation of a capitalist society required the creation of an economic society, as well as (or even more than) the formation of performers that advance industrialization, and this progression has been observed worldwide within decentralized societies, a special type of society. Therefore, the issues of economic history are present in ascertaining when and how the formation of this economic society progressed. Also, the core of economic history is examining how the performers and conditions for industrialization were prepared under these circumstances.

Chapter 2
Before the Emergence of Economic Society

2.1 The Birth of a "Decentralized Society"

The process in which "decentralized society" formed was slow everywhere. In Western Europe, it appeared mostly in the eighth and ninth centuries. However, this required more than 400 years after the collapse of the Roman Empire and over the course of several historical events. Those included the large fluctuations that took place in Europe after the fourth century, the invasions of the Roman Empire by German tribes, the formation of German tribal states, and the Islamic takeover of the Mediterranean Sea and Southern Europe, and certainly this process did not take place all at once. Considering the era when the German tribes learned of state-formation systems and literacy through their contact with Rome and came into contact with a universal religion called Christianity, even in Western Europe the formation of decentralized society had 500-plus years of transition.

In the case of Japan, between the period in which the ancient state was established and the "decentralized society" was formed (which we can view as the Sengoku Warring States Period), there was a period of approximately a millennium, in which 400 years, counted from the period when the nucleus for the change to a "decentralized society" formed (viewed as the late Heian Period – more on this later), is a "transition period." Moreover, in Japan, based on the fact that the governmental system adopted during the state formation period was imported from the Sui and Tang dynasties in China – the most complete of the ancient states – and its own nature as an Asian irrigation agricultural society, elements of an "ancient state" remained in the political structure for a long time. Until these were eliminated and a "decentralized" control structure was established, there were repeated compromise and conflict among societies with uncertain realities in the ancient framework. In some cases, unstable and contradiction-ridden political forces were organized, and fleeting moments of stability were attained under some of these systems, but no fundamental solutions were seen, which led to the state of anarchy in the fifteenth

A. Hayami, *Japan's Industrious Revolution*, Studies in Economic History,
DOI 10.1007/978-4-431-55142-3_2

and sixteenth centuries. Moreover – as will be explained later – during that period, the formation of economic society made strides locally, but the nature of a new political force that would resolve this state of anarchy could not simultaneously take hold of the formation of economic society. In this regard, it differs from the process in which feudal society formed in Western Europe. In contrast to the formation of feudal society in Western Europe, which was premised on the total decline of economic activity, in Japan, the successive nationwide governments created by Oda Nobunaga, Toyotomi Hideyoshi, and Tokugawa Ieyasu, in the last two decades of sixteenth century and the first decade of the seventeenth century had to factor in the presence of economic society from the onset and how they would respond to it. In these regards, the differences between Western Europe and Japan's historical experiences become apparent.

This chapter will examine how Japan incorporated the "ancient society" framework prior to the formation of economic society in the aforementioned process and traversed a historical path riddled with contradictions, and the qualities that were required for an economy under this system.

2.2 State Formation in Ancient Japan

The period spanning the sixth and seventh centuries was one when the Japanese archipelago finally started to move toward national unification, along with incorporating Buddhism as a universal religion and literacy as an important means for transmitting culture. Wet-paddy rice agriculture had already entered Japan earlier, and irrigation facilities had been placed on terraced land and in the plains, but state formation was under way under the sole force among the numerous regional powers that subjugated the Yamato region. In this case, one must remember that in China the Sui and Tang dynasties were politically and culturally in their full glory as the most complete forms of the ancient state. Japan inevitably had to respond in some fashion to this brilliance. Unable to choose between the two extremes of complete absorption or outright rejection, Japan ultimately had no choice other than to form a state using a somewhat Japanized *ritsuryō* (legal) system of government based on the Chinese framework modeled after Sui and Tang governmental systems.

As a form of state organization, the *ritsuryō* system was an extremely elaborate form of government, and it constituted a powerful national force. The system did not limit itself to the central bureaucracy; the organization of state control was also cast like a net over the provinces; and people were no longer able to escape from it. Agricultural production was greatly impacted, and the construction of numerous irrigation projects and the planned reclamation of flatlands carried out by the *ritsuryō* government naturally led to an increase in agricultural production.

2.3 Land System under the Ancient State

In particular, the land system under the *ritsuryō* system operated on the premise of state ownership where "all of the land in the realm belonged to the sovereign," and taxes were collected from leasehold farmers in accordance with this rationale. The *handen* allocation system (Japanese adaptation of the Chinese equal field system) established under the Taihō Code (701) was adopted as the system which most effectively collected taxes and enforced the basic principles of the state ownership system. However, according to recent research, this method could not be seen as uniformly implemented throughout Japan, and it must be kept in mind that its powers were limited to the Kinai region (Central area; including Yamashiro, Yamato, Settsu, Kawachi, and Izumi Provinces (*kuni*)) and regions under the influence of the *ritsuryō* government authority (for example, the areas around provincial capitals), and that by the ninth century it was no longer in force.

From a technical standpoint, this system was based on the premise that accurate and detailed land and household registries would be compiled, which required trained government officials possessing advanced investigative skills. There is considerable doubt as to whether Japan at that time was actually capable of preparing such officials nationwide (Torao 1961, pp. 415–452).

However, most important is that the *handen* allocation system was becoming difficult to implement internally. A shortage of land and technical difficulties due to an increase in the peasant population were originally listed as the causes for the breakdown of the *handen* allocation system, but as there is no compelling evidence that there was an increase in the population, particularly during this period, it cannot be vaguely assumed that the population increased. Instead, it has been pointed out that the amount of nobles' lands, bureaucratic lands, meritorious award lands, imperially granted lands, and temple and shrine lands awarded mainly to the upper classes and to temples and shrines increased alongside the development of the *ritsuryō* government, resulting in a shortage of lands to distribute to the peasantry. Consequently, land shortages primarily occurred in the Kinai area.

The upper classes and temples and shrines received their land grants legally, but in addition, the *sanzeisshin-no-hō* in 723 (a law permitting three generations to privately own land after it has been reclamed), followed by the *kondeneinenshizai-no-hō* in 743 (a law permitting eternal exclusive right of *konden* (reclaimed rice fields) in perpetuity) allowed them to amass land, and as these laws in effect permitted private ownership of land, they were by nature entirely incompatible with the *handen* allocation system, which was based on the principle of total state ownership. The legal ownership of land within just a century of the adoption of the principle of state ownership most clearly demonstrates the nature of the existence of the ancient state in Japan.

Thus, the *handen* allocation system did not become an established presence and was merely a land system implemented for a relatively brief period in some areas. However, the fact that the *handen* allocation system was no longer enforced does not mean that the *ritsuryō* system collapsed. The *handen* allocation system was a land system originally created through the complete implementation of state ownership of land. Therefore, the principle of state ownership of land remained. Land still belonged to the state, and the peasants who leased the land were obligated to pay levies. The levy structure with provincial governors (*kokushi*) on the top, district managers (*gunshi*) in the middle, and administrative village heads (*satoosa*) at the bottom survived for quite a long time. Also, strictly speaking it is difficult to call the so-called phenomenon of privatization "private ownership," as there were various restrictions, and a great majority of "private lands" had levies imposed on them. However, the taxation rate set under the *ritsuryō* system was not that high – around 1.5 bundles of rice per 1,000 m^2 of rice field, approximately 3% of the harvest; rather, there were cases where the miscellaneous levies imposed by provincial officials were a greater burden. Therefore, had the *handen* allocation system not been implemented, and had it become customary for peasant families to cultivate the same plot of land generation after generation, production would have increased to a certain degree, which would have generated a surplus. In this sense, people had to choose either between the *handen* allocation system and private land ownership.

Why did the frenzy over private land ownership by capital aristocrats, powerful provincial clans, and temples and shrines become a problem during this period? Had the ideals of the Taika Reforms (645) been implemented as intended, there is no way that these forces should have been able to privately own land. In this regard, there are conspicuous differences between ideals and reality. This cannot be understood without thinking about the circumstances in which Japan was placed from the Asuka and Nara Periods through the Heian Period. During this period, Japan finally escaped from its primordial state and had sophisticated "cultural" experiences. Naturally, only limited segments of society were able to bask in this, but now urban life had begun, peace was maintained under the framework of the *ritsuryō* system, writing was used, temple and shrine structures were constructed one after another, "literature" came into being, and poetry and arts became a part of their lives.

From the era of the *Man'yōshū* (Anthology of Ten Thousand Leaves), the *Kojiki* (Chronicle of Ancient Matters), and the *Nihon shoki* (Chronicles of Japan) up to the era of *Genji-monogatari*, it was as though Japanese society came out of the darkness and into the light. When the cultural artifacts from the Asuka Period and earlier are compared to those later, one can immediately sense that the fault line between these two periods is large. The primary bearers of this spiritual culture were the capital aristocrats, and their commitment to culture required a commensurate material foundation. Moreover, the income set by the *ritsuryō* was insufficient, so at a time when they lacked other means to obtain income, the only way they could accomplish this was through private land ownership.

In addition, the autocratic control possessed by the ancient state in Japan cannot be said to have been as powerful as that in other ancient East Asian societies. At the very least, the state was not configured so that all power was concentrated in a single ruler. The *ritsuryō* system was a system that permitted the maintenance of control as a system, but the power held by the emperor, the supreme authority under the *ritsuryō*, did not belong to the emperor or empress themselves in substance; rather, it was maintained by the aristocratic forces that supported them. This was certainly the case when the Fujiwara clan monopolized the regency and chancellorship, but this was by no means stable and fell into decline with the appearance of the *insei* (retired emperors). *Zuryō* (the highest provincial officials) from the middle aristocratic ranks possessed a certain degree of actual power. In other words, Japan did not adopt a system where power was concentrated in one royal house or in one lineage. These circumstances operated as a condition that was forced to recognize private land ownership by aristocrats and temples and shrines, even though this was clearly at odds with public ownership, the principle of the *ritsuryō* system. This type of private ownership of land is what we call a *shōen* (on the emergence of this type of estate, see Morris 1999, pp. 224–235), and we will examine this below.

2.4 Structure of the *Shōen*

The word *shōen* has been in existence for a long time. However, from the Meiji Period onward, confusion has ensued because Japanese historians translated the European historical terms "manor," "*Grundherrschaft*" or "*seigneurie*" as *shōen*. The *shōen* in European history is an entirely different system from that in Japanese history. To prevent misunderstandings, it is probably better to understand these two – European and Japanese – as separate systems with virtually no similarities.

First, judging by the circumstances of its creation, on the one hand the *shōen* system in Japan required the ancient state framework of the *ritsuryō* system. The *ritsuryō* and *shōen* systems were mutually contradictory, yet the *shōen* system required the *ritsuryō* system in a complementary capacity. In Europe, the *shōen* system was a land system under the feudal system, and the terms "*shōen* system" and "feudal system" were used to understand a single society from different angles. However, in Japan, the terms "feudal system" and "*ritsuryō* system" are not phrases referring to a single society. There is room for disagreement here, but instead it is better to say that these expressions refer to completely distinct societies. As such, equating the *shōen* system with feudalism, feudalism with serfdom, and serfdom with medievalism does not apply to Japan.

Second, in Europe, the *shōen* was a system of land control, and the proprietor was the sole sovereign over that land. His control extended to everything: for example, land, buildings, residents, livestock, and produce. However, this was not the case in Japan, and with the exception of the early self-reclaimed *shōen*, the proprietor's rights consisted of the right to acquire a fixed percentage of the *nengu* generated by the land, something that can hardly be called land control. Therefore, looking at the relationship between the proprietors and the peasants, in Europe the peasants practically existed as indentured serfs and were subject to various legal and status restrictions, but in Japan, there were no status restrictions, and there was no concept of people who were free and those who were not. One reason for defined status in Europe is that direct management of the *shōen* had a great deal of weight and had the specific objective of securing labor, in contrast to Japan, where there was no direct management of *shōen* lands (or if there was, it was on a small scale and unnecessary). While the *handen* allocation system continued, peasants were registered in household and population registers (*koseki*) and regarded as "the recognized," but when that was discontinued, the point of creating household and population registers was lost. Under the *shōen* system, the relationship between the *shōen* proprietor and the peasants became less and less one of personal control.

2.5 Categories of *Shōen*

Shōen can be placed into three categories based on the circumstances of their formation:

1. Self-Reclaimed *Shōen*: These were created through large-scale reclamation efforts by temples and shrines around the eighth and ninth centuries based on the law permitting ownership of developed land in perpetuity. The development of the Hokuriku region by the Tōdaiji temple is a well-known example. Generally, large areas of undeveloped land were demarcated and land reclamation proceeded through the introduction of resources and labor, and securing labor was a major issue. In some cases, drifters (people who were not registered in a family register, not so much people who were actually drifting) were sent to the *shōen* and forced to settle there, so proprietors were relatively powerful particularly at these types of *shōen*.
2. Levy-Exempt *Shōen*: Originally, temples and shrines were awarded a portion of the levies the state imposed on the people as official taxes. In order to avoid the complications which arose from the *kokuga* (provincial headquarters) collecting the levies before giving them to the temples and shrines, the system was changed so that the temples and shrines could collect these levies directly. Additionally, in the eleventh and twelfth centuries, the object of collections came to refer to specific lands, and it is here that we see the creation of the *shōen*. These were primarily in the Kinai area.
3. Donated *Shōen*: These were created by wealthy resident landowners (such as those who comprised the district, village, and local official classes under the *ritsuryō* system) donating their rights to collect annual levies to court aristocrats. *Shōen* proprietor rights were divided and maintained among several layers in order to permit wealthy provincial landowners, who served as intermediaries for the provincial governors, to make illegal donations within the *ritsuryō* system. There were many secular (not temple and shrines owned) *shōen* in this category, and they reached their peak from the end of the eleventh century and through the twelfth century.

In actuality, the three *shōen* categories mentioned above were mixed and transformed, so they cannot be neatly categorized in this manner. Even viewed from their individual characters, the differences among the categories did not endure for an extended period.

2.6 The Progress of *Shōen* Formation

To what degree did *shōen* formation progress? In terms of spatial expansion, there was a considerable degree of progress in the areas surrounding Kyoto and Nara, where the proprietor class resided. In Iga Province, two-thirds of arable land became some sort of *shōen* during the eleventh century; and in the early twelfth century, at least 80% of the six districts in northern Kii Province were turned into *shōen*, with the two northernmost districts near Temple Kōyasan turned entirely into *shōen*. Also, in the mid-eleventh century, the Kōfukuji temple in Nara owned 151 *shōen*, or 2,358 *chō* (5,778 acres) across 15 districts in Yamato Province. As such, there was aggressive *shōen* formation in the Kinai and surrounding areas, and conversely, peripheral areas held little land. However, it is likely that the percentage of *shōen* holdings decreased the further one went from the Kinai area.

On the other hand, the development of vertical ownership rights within the *shōen* appeared in the form of tax-exempt *shōen*. Originally, land was divided into taxable and tax-exempt under the *ritsuryō* system, and rice fields held by temples, as well as those held by court bureaucrats, fell into the latter category. As the significance of private land ownership grew, aristocratic lands and meritoriously awarded lands also became tax-exempt, and from the mid-ninth century, a system was created where *shōen* lands could be made tax-exempt through a prescribed process. First, *shōen* landowners petitioned the central government for tax-exempt status. When the central government recognized the landowner's claims and accepted the petition, it then ordered provincial officials to investigate whether the claims stated in the petition were accurate. Upon verification, the petition was approved. Here, since the responsible government agencies were the *Dajōkan* (the Grand Council of State) and the *Minbushō* (the Ministry of Taxation), the document approving tax-exempt status was called "*kanshō-fu-shō*" (tax-exempted *shōen* through the document by high ministries). Moreover, the authority of provincial governors expanded during the eleventh century, and they were now able to grant tax-exempt privileges on their own authority (*kokumenshō*, or *shōen* granted tax-exempt status by a provincial governor), broadening the range of *shōen*.

Shōen receiving tax-exempt status represented a substantial change in the *shōen* under the state system. This was because the *ritsuryō* government lost an equivalent amount of income. Therefore, for the *ritsuryō* government, increasing of tax-exempt lands was akin to digging its own grave. On top of that, this was accomplished through legal means by high-ranking aristocratic officials in the *ritsuryō* government, as well as temples and shrines. On occasion, measures were taken against this type of destructive act toward the *ritsuryō* system and through issuing the *shōen-seirirei* (order to consolidate *shōen*) and establishing the *shōen-kenkeijo* (office for the investigation of *shōen* documents), *shōen* of uncertain status were seized by the government. However, the opposite held true as well – *shōen* approved through these measures were now officially recognized as privately owned.

When one considers the peak of the *shōen* system in the eleventh and twelfth centuries, the *ritsuryō* system and *shōen* system were land systems based on mutually incompatible principles, yet they were in an extremely peculiar relationship where court aristocrats both managed these systems and owned land under them. The aristocrats held a fixed position and office under the *ritsuryō* system, while bringing the *ritsuryō* system to the brink of disaster by legalizing acts such as promoting the conversion of land into *shōen*, as well as making them tax-exempt. The Heian court aristocrats were this type of contradictory, unstable presence, and furthermore, court culture blossomed.

2.7 The Character of *Shōen* Ownership Rights

The description above shows that the *shōen* system inherited its ownership rights from the land and peasant control rights held by the state under the *ritsuryō* system. This strongly defined the character of the *shōen* system, as the *shōen* were created through legal means under the *ritsuryō* system. *Shōen* landowners received the *nengu* from the *shōen* as a form of profit, and collection of *nengu* was not linked to a responsibility or obligation to manage their holdings or to provide for the protection of its residents. Most likely, not a single *shōen* owner actually set foot inside their own *shōen*. In addition, land owned by nobles in particular was subject to extreme fluctuations due to inheritance, sale, and transfer. Also, in the process of donating land or making it tax-exempt, a portion of the ownership rights was transferred to another layer, and as is often stated, this created a stratified relationship of ownership rights: *honjo* (patron/highest guarantor of a shōen)→*ryōke* (proprietor)→*azukaridokoro* (custodian), and *shōen* ownership rights became stratified.

Thus, the right of a *shōen* landowner to receive *nengu* from the *shōen* is a transformation of the tax collection rights possessed by the state under the *ritsuryō* system, and it was not something that formed the territory, so the maintenance of domestic order was an absolute premise for collecting *nengu*. Then, this work was primarily handled by the *ritsuryō* government. In other words, it is not as though the *shōen* landowner had some kind of defined enforcement powers. At best, officials were sent to manage the *shōen*, and it is no exaggeration to say that they relied on the *ritsuryō* government for almost all enforcement powers. While the *shōen* system contradicted the *ritsuryō* system, on the other hand the conditions which required them to coexist were here. Therefore, in actuality the *ritsuryō* system and the *shōen* system were not separate, independent entities; a single system was formed through this complex entanglement. Also, it is precisely this system that survived as the framework for political control in Japan during the 900-year period from the Taika Reforms to the anarchy of the Sengoku Period.

2.8 Formation of Warrior Governments

Since the creation of the Kamakura Shogunate, warrior authority became a new force to use this framework. Also, along with the weakening of the *ritsuryō* government's political power, a class of wealthy provincial landowners appeared, further complicating the conflicts between the various social forces surrounding the *shōen*. However, the system itself survived since both the Kamakura and Muromachi Bakufu were unable to abolish this system and replace it with a new system of control. The abolition of this system became possible for the first time through the rise of the governments of Oda Nobunaga and Toyotomi Hideyoshi, which discontinued the *ritsuryō* and *shōen* systems simultaneously after the anarchy of the Sengoku Period.

The creation of the Kamakura Bakufu can be understood in the following manner. The high point of the *shōen* system during the eleventh and twelfth centuries meant the appearance of a type of void beyond the reach of any government authority. While the financial foundations of the *ritsuryō* government were being undermined, the *shōen* acquired not only tax-exemption privileges but also the right to forbid government officials from entering its estates. A broad interpretation of these rights led to the right to exclude police intervention. When the authority of the *ritsuryō* system fell into decline, a new force was formed to fill the void. This was no longer the force of law, as in the *ritsuryō* system, but a force based on more direct power, i.e., military force. Then, between the two forces which formed this system – the Minamoto and Taira clans – a new form of government was founded by the Minamoto, who were primarily based in the Eastern Provinces.

2.9 Kamakura Bakufu

The matter of how to position the appearance of the Kamakura Bakufu in economic history is certainly not an easy one.[1] We can no longer directly link the "feudal" world to the creation of the shogunate, as Rai Sanyō, a littérateur in the Edo Period, in his famous historical story "Nihon Gaishi" (an unofficial history of Japan) had likened the Kamakura Period to ancient China, which divided the administration in two: direct controlled areas and remote "feudal" areas. As he was a man of *belles lettres,* a million copies of the book were published and influenced historical awareness. Not only that, if we are able to use the framework discussed thus far, we could even say that the creation of the shogunate substantially intended no immediate

[1] The best book on the Kamakura Bakufu is Mass (1976).

changes to the social structure. The reason that historians from the Meiji Period onward viewed the establishment of the Kamakura Bakufu as the creation of feudalism is based on an understanding of feudalism as loyalty relationships between lord and retainer mediated by land grants and considered land grants to *jitō* (military estate steward) appointments. However, at least when the *shōen* were first created, the *gokenin* were awarded land as territory. On the level of individual *shōen*, they were merely awarded status as a *shōen* officers known as a *jitō*. Originally, *shōen* had officers assigned by the actual *shōen* proprietor, and they managed the *shōen* and collected the *nengu*. Many of these newly emerged military forces had their origins as capable peasants or from the *shōen* officer classes, and there were also *shōen jitō* who were appointed from among their ranks. The authority of the *jitō* was no different from that of an ordinary *shōen* officer, and the only difference was that they had police powers within the *shōen*. (Also, constables known as *shugo* (military provincial governor) were placed in each province to supervise these *jitō* as police powers). Therefore, in the beginning, the *jitō* managed the *shōen*, and their job was to make sure that the *nengu* from the *shōen* was delivered to the *shōen* proprietor as prescribed. Naturally, he received a fixed percentage as compensation for his duties as *jitō*, but at any rate this did not mean some kind of "territory."

Also, the relationship between the Kamakura Bakufu and the *ritsuryō* government was by no means an "either–or" situation. The shogunate likely would have had no difficulty staging a military overthrow of the *ritsuryō* government. Nonetheless, they took great pains to avoid this, so much so that they were unable to topple the *ritsuryō* government even during the Jōkyu Disturbance (1221, a feud between the emperor and Kamakura Bakufu). This should serve as evidence that the *bakufu* itself still lacked the ability to govern the state on its own.

Even looking at the composition of the *bakufu*, its various organs served to manage the private assets of the shogun's family, and at most regulated the relationships with the *gokenin* (vassals). Their sole legal code, the Jōei Code, was compiled as warrior law and as a counterweight to the *ritsuryō*, but compared to the *ritsuryō* its contents were considerably simplified and had limited applicability. By no means could it be simply deemed "national law." In somewhat extreme terms, the *bakufu* used its military powers to assume the public security abilities that the *ritsuryō* government lost, and they were in a complementary relationship. In addition, the Kamakura Bakufu originally began as a regional faction. In other words, the *bakufu* was based on the relationship between the shogun and *gokenin,* and while it did cover the Kantō region and its surrounding areas, it certainly was not a nationwide organization. In particular, in western Japan there were numerous warriors – the non-*gokenin* who did not submit to the shogunate's authority. There was virtually no relationship between them and the shogunate, except during the Mongol invasions.

As such, the Kamakura Bakufu had only partial authority, and was not strong enough to stand alone as a national government without the *ritsuryō* government, all the more reason that it cannot be directly linked to a feudal government. There are even recent studies that view this period as an "ancient" period based on the relative strength of the shogun and *shikken* (shogunal regent). When these circumstances are taken together, even the "Kamakura Period" label we casually use is an expression that is easily misunderstood.

Then, is it true that the formation of the Kamakura shogunate lent no substantial change to Japanese history? We shall examine this problem below by looking at the nature of the *jitō*.

2.10 *Jitō*

First, as stated above, the *jitō* did not rely on their status within the *shōen*. With a virtual monopoly on military and police power, they soon discovered that there was no one to oppose then within the *shōen*. In addition, when military force was organized into a single system, it naturally came to possess its own "culture." Just like the noble and aristocratic classes of the Heian court, they learned about life in Kyoto and Kamakura, and as their opportunities to absorb culture gradually increased, they demanded greater incomes. At that point, they first targeted the *nengu* from the *shōen*. They did not remit the prescribed *nengu* and kept it for themselves. Of course, the *shōen* seigneurs decried these actions as illegal confiscations and dispatched their *shōen* officers to claim the *nengu*, but to no avail. For the seigneurs, the *nengu* was practically their sole source of income, and the seizure of this income meant that they would immediately go bankrupt. Realizing that they had no direct means to fight this, the landowners' next step was to appeal to the shogunate. The shogunate did adjudicate the seigneurs' complaints, and did not always necessarily rule in favor of their retainers, the *gokenin*. This is also a salient fact which speaks to the relationship between the shogunate and nobles/aristocrats (and the *ritsuryō* government they belonged to). Ultimately, in some ways the shogunate needed the *ritsuryō* government.

The appearance of the *jitōuke*– a compromise system – is an example of the result of a ruling. This was a system where the *jitōuke* is responsible for collecting the fixed *nengu* and is able to keep whatever is left over. This system recognized the rights of both parties, and became quite common during the Kamakura Period. However, the *jitō* sought to further expand its authority, and when they started to be delinquent with the *nengu* they were responsible for, *shōen* lands were divided between the former proprietor and the *jitō* through a direct compromise (*wayo*) between the two parties. Another possibility was to do the same thing through a shogunate ruling called a *shitajichūbun* (where the *shōen* was physically divided). Ownership by the *jitō* increased through this type of expansion of power, and approximated a "subject–vassal relationship based on the award of land." However, as time went by and Japan entered the Muromachi Period, warrior invasions of the *shōen* further increased in scale, so *shugouke* (contracts to manage the *shōen*) issued by the *shugo* took the form of *hanzei* (equally dividing the *shōennengu*).

This type of ownership by the *jitō*, and later the *shugo*, did not occur only on the *shōen*, but on the *kokugaryō* (provincial domains) as well. Also, the establishment of *zaichiryōshu* control by the *jitō* class or equivalent wealthy provincial seigneurs were seen on the fringes of the *shōen* system. Had this type of control spread uniformly throughout the country, it might have been possible to label it a "decentralized society" as a new framework of control. However, things had yet to progress to that level during the Kamakura Period. In the end, the *ritsuryō* and *shōen* systems remained, and the shogunate itself was not "feudalistic" in nature.

2.11 The Peasantry

Now, what were the economic and social conditions of the peasants during this period between the *handen* allocation system and the *shōen* system? As mentioned earlier, the *shōen* proprietors were a type of parasite living off of land rents and were unconcerned with the condition of the peasants or production on the *shōen*. As such, there are no written documents pertaining to these matters. Since the peasants were also virtually illiterate, one cannot expect that they kept any records of their own.

Under the *handen* allocation system, household and population registers were compiled, fragments of which still exist today. An examination of these household registers shows that peasant families were rather large, and included numerous cohabitating family members and slaves, so there were many households with upwards of 20 to 30 members. Also, based on the fact that this family structure was seen even in the *ninbetsuaratame* (census) taken during the early seventeenth century (a much later period) we can assume that peasant families under the *shōen* system were large. From the seigneur's viewpoint, key peasant families were called *tato* (land manager) during the tenth and eleventh centuries. Originally, the word *tato* meant "land," but its meaning later changed to refer to the landholders. In the late Heian Period, standard peasants came to be called *myōshu* (local landholders). These peasant families were called *myōshu* because they obtained cultivation and possession rights on specific parcels of land by clearing it, purchasing it, or cultivating it for generations, and the parcel assumed the name of the peasant family. being called *myōden* (fields with names). As such, the *myōshu* included those who held large plots of land to those who owned just a little, and they additionally included peasants with strong military elements, since the peasantry and military were still not separated. Agriculture managed by these *myōshu* was referred to as "*myōden* administration," a management style where the direct descendants of the family that owned the land used subordinate labor from their extended family, as well as low-ranking persons known as *nago*, *fudai*, and *ge'nin*, and it is generally assumed that they extensively cultivated comparatively large tracts of land (regardless of whether it was *shōen* land). However, it would be a mistake to broadly describe agricultural management during this period in terms of this type of *myōden* management. In reality, there were also small-scale *myōshu* who relied primarily on family labor, tenant farmers who leased land from the *myōshu*, and subcontract tenant farmers who leased land from other tenant farmers, and naturally the lands they managed were unmistakably small in scale. Rather, we should willingly accept the fact that agricultural management during this period lacked specificity in terms of scale and technology. For reasons that will be explained later, agricultural management during this period was far too diverse to create a single image from fragmentary historical documents. The fact that the scale and technology of Japanese agriculture attained a certain "form" and reached a certain "standard" from the Edo Period onward is in and of itself a product of history, and by no means was this situation throughout Japanese history.

Several peasant families gathered to form a village (*mura*). Villages had various origins – some naturally formed in order to maintain an agricultural livelihood, while others were created as a result of land reclamation – and they were not uniform in scale either. At the very least, we can say that a *shōen* did not correspond to a village. Particularly in cases where *shōen* were created as a result of donations, they were aggregates of land with artificially delineated boundaries or with a specific relationship, and there were many cases where they did not overlap with villages. Even for the peasants, the land they cultivated was certainly not limited to a single *shōen*, and were often mixed in with parcels that belonged to other *shōen* or *kokugaryō* or those judged as terra nullius . Even for the so-called *kintōmyō* (*myōden* fields of equal size) observed in the *shōen* in the Kinai region during the late Heian Period, it should not be automatically assumed that the arable land retained by the peasants was equally partitioned as it was for the *Hufenver* peasants in Europe.

Our information on the agricultural technology of the period is also extremely limited. Iron agricultural implements appear to have been widely available, but along with livestock, their possession largely likely did not extend beyond the *myōshu* class. Cultivation did not yet have the intensiveness seen in the Edo Period. Intensiveness with irrigated agriculture and an extensiveness brought forth by the character of labor were demands in mutually opposite directions, and it could be said that cultivation was in a state where it could not develop in either direction.

2.12 The Economy of the *Shōen* System

The economy of the *shōen* system can be generally expressed by Fig. 2.1 (compare and contrast with Fig. 4.1, the conceptual diagram of the economic structure in the Edo Period, in Chapter 4). The largest element to flow through this society was none

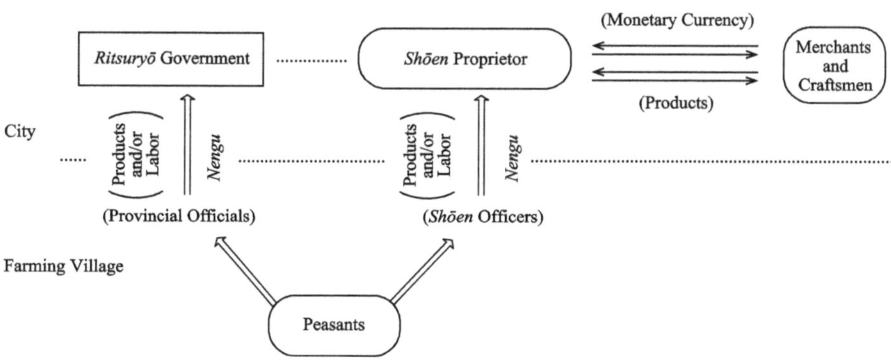

Fig. 2.1 The Flows of Goods and Currency before the Early Modern Period

other than the *nengu* from the *shōen*, which was produced by the peasants and delivered to the seigneurs in product form. In actuality, the *shōen nengu* that appeared in the records show that an extremely diverse range of products were delivered on very specific dates. It is clear that besides the expected rice and grains, the items that the urban dwelling seigneur class required in their everyday lives, such as food, seafood products, seasonings, clothing (and the materials for clothing), fuel, and building materials, were supplemented via *nengu* in kind (as opposed to monetary payments). Some of the items replenished outside of the *nengu* system were daily essentials, but merchants took care of luxury items and imported goods. Also, some *shōen* had specialty products, and it is assumed that part of the *nengu* was delivered to the market via merchants and artisans. However, the everyday lives of the landholder class (including the seigneurs themselves, their families, servants, merchants who dealt with the landholders, craftsmen, and intellectuals) relied almost entirely on in-kind *nengu* payments, so it can be assumed that agricultural products were directly consumed. Also, markets were created based primarily on luxury items, imported goods, some specialty items, and fresh foodstuffs from nearby farming villages, and monetary currency was in circulation as a medium for exchange, but as illustrated in the diagram, this pertained to a portion of the urban privileged class and was virtually irrelevant to the peasants. As such, entrusting lifestyle essentials to in-kind *nengu,* their transportation – particularly long-distance transport from frontier regions – was a major problem. At a time when transportation methods were limited, more than anything the maintenance of law and order was required in order to safely transport the in-kind *nengu* according to specifications, and it was necessary to handle delays and backlogs in *nengu* transport with national laws. Since this was the responsibility of the *ritsuryō* government, not the *shōen* landowners, it was necessary for the *ritsuryō* government to be strong in this regard as well. Gradually, professional shipping contractors appeared to handle transportation matters, and they had names such as *toi*, *toimaru*, or *tsuya*. Since they primarily relied on water transport, these contractors based themselves in areas with easy access to water.

2.13 Purpose of Production

Under the conditions described above, the peasants had no choice but to limit their production objectives to *nengu* and self-sufficiency. These two objectives meant that the goods they produced were mandatory. The *nengu* was mandatory in the sense that failure to deliver these goods would result in punishments, and self-sufficiency was mandatory in the sense that they would starve if they did not produce crops. Moreover, for the servant labor which comprised the majority of direct producers, mandatory production meant that they were whipped even more. What kind of relationship do producers have with their behaviors of production (i.e., their labor) when production is motivated by compulsion? People are likely to view labor as nothing more than unavoidable toil under these kinds of circumstances. An ethos where labor is accorded a positive meaning is unable to develop in such a society. Quite the opposite, people are likely to feel that labor is a pain and attempt to escape it by doing the bare minimum. Here, not the slightest bit of effort is made on the part of the producers to improve production technology and organization and make greater production a reality. Production merely continues as it always has, and the peasants have nothing more than a passive relationship with production.

In addition, the seigneurs made no effort to increase production either. By nature, the *shōen* proprietor's rights were the ones to a portion of the *nengu*, and these rights were divided and stratified, so it is not as though the seigneur possessed a stretch of land. Therefore, the *shōen* proprietors could not expect production beyond maintaining the status quo. The *shōen* seigneurs were unable to generate more *nengu* horizontally (i.e. by improving agricultural production), so their method to obtain more income was to vertically attain a better position within the *ritsuryō* system and acquire more *shōen* through donations, transfers, or purchases. Even if the seigneurs attempted to improve agriculture on the *shōen*, their territorial possessions were fragmented, and in a state where ownership rights were stratified at a single *shōen*, the extent to which ownership rights could be exercised was limited to the customary collection of *nengu*. Therefore, neither producers nor masters had any motivation to increase production, and production standards can be seen stalled at a low level for an extended period.

Not only that, it is also conceivable that production amounts actually even decreased. In other words, when the *ritsuryō* government was first created, the necessary conditions for agricultural production were established, and in particular, the construction of flood control irrigation projects in the plains held great significance in bringing about an increase in production. Yet, once the fiscal and administrative capabilities of the *ritsuryō* government began to decline, it became difficult to maintain and repair these facilities. Also, records frequently show that farmland in the plains were abandoned, so it is assumed that the center of production shifted toward less productive valleys and small basins (however, this was only to the extent that local peasants were able to maintain irrigation systems). If this situation were commonplace, overall production unmistakably would have contracted instead. Therefore, we can also assume that the population shrank. Production and population, or although indeterminate, production capacity, will increase over an extremely long period. For example, if we look at the very long historical perspective, all of these indices would "increase." However, this does not mean that "increase" exists permanently. It may be acceptable to recognize these increases as latent potential, but it is the conditions in the respective eras that determine whether the increase will become a reality. There is no reason for us to assume that these "increases" were present under the *shōen* system.

2.14 The Absence of Economic Society and the Nature of *Nengu*

When economic activity in overall society is an extremely inactive state – particularly in regards to production – it does not stand to reason that people will base their behavior on economic rationalism. Consequently, circumstances where production favors a particular model in pursuit of maximum efficiency also did not transpire. When explaining that the images present-day historians have of the peasants from this period are highly diverse, and are based on records, we must bear in mind that they lived under these kinds of conditions.

It is precisely this lax state of economic activity and stagnation in production technology that were the basic features characterizing production under the *shōen* system. There were virtually no changes in productivity and no fluctuations in population or total production in either the short or long term. The inclusion of servant labor into peasant households kept marriage and birth rates throughout the entire peasant class low, maintaining a balance with the death rate. Naturally, living standards were low, and likely approached subsistence levels. The death rate was much higher than it was during the early Edo Period (which we are able to measure), and average life expectancies were likely short. (Refer to Chapter 4 for an analysis on this). In particular, the living standards of the *nago* (hereditary servant), *fudai,* and *ge'nin* who belonged to the servant class were undoubtedly extremely low.

Another conspicuous fact that characterized the economy under this *shōen* system can be found in the nature of the *nengu*. The *shōen* seigneurs collected the *nengu* from the peasants mainly in order to satisfy their own private consumption. As long as this was the case, the *nengu* flowed as a unidirectional transfer of goods within the framework of the seigneur's private household economy. Therefore, the nature of the *nengu* was that of a form of rent, not a tax. However, under the *ritsuryō* system, the *shōen-nengu* took over as the tax that the peasants were obligated to pay the state, and the problems inherent in the history of this period can be found lurking in the fact that taxes were converted to rent under this ancient state system. This was a contradiction from the logic of the ancient state system. What were the conditions that presumed to choose this contradiction and make it possible? Also, what does the rise of the warrior government, which further complicated matters, tell us?

2.15 Conditions for the Survival of the *Shōen* Economy

One more question that must be added is how this system managed to survive for close to a millennium despite being an unstable framework fraught with contradictions. Assuming that the *pro forma* changes in government were a kind of "dynasty change drama" and not a change in the framework itself, the fact that this type of unstable framework was able to survive for a long time needs to be adequately explained.

In response to this fundamental question, we shall first look at foreign relations during this period. Japan during the Sui and Tang dynasties almost unilaterally incorporated many things from the Korean peninsula and continental China, but a sort of instability started from around the time of the decline of the Tang Empire in the early tenth century. Also, the Korean peninsula was unified under the Koguryo in the tenth century, but after that, relations with Japan were relatively distant. From around this time, Japan was relatively uninfluenced by the tensions that occurred in foreign relations; therefore, it primarily entrusted its history to domestic events. Of course, there were many exceptions, and foreign interactions were not strictly restricted the way they were during the Edo Period. However, aside from one major exception, the fact of the matter is that Japan did not perceive foreign countries as a threat from this time until around the sixteenth century. With the help of Japan's insular environment, this became an extremely important factor in allowing this unstable condition to continue for a long time. Obviously, the sole exception was the Mongol invasions (1274 and 1281).

As expected, domestic tensions were also visible during this time, and the Kamakura shogunate organized even the *non-gokenin* (warriors not paying homage to the Kamamura shogunate) class into a military structure. From the onset, it would have been natural for a single government to promote this type of organization on a national level. However, in reality, this type of mobilization system conversely served to hasten the downfall of the shogunate. This also shows that the Kamakura shogunate did not have a foundation as a robust political authority that reigned over the entire nation.

Thus, the lack of foreign relations is evident compared to, for example, Europe of the same period, which meant that an unstable, contradiction-filled situation continued for a long period, and at least in foreign relations, the need to quickly outgrow this system was likely not recognized.

Next, lax economic activity must be considered. Economic activity evenly permeating all classes of society means that within this society people (or classes) who successfully seize economic opportunities are founded and obtain a form of economic power. Here, when the classes that have gained power are politically subordinated classes, some form of social fluctuation may occur. However, when economic activity is markedly lax, and those who can engage in it and obtain economic power are extremely limited, and these people already possess political power, social fluctuation linked to economy is unlikely to occur. This is certainly true for the era of the *shōen*. Put into extreme terms, the history that unfolded was nothing more than a kind of "dynasty change drama."

2.16 The Muromachi Period

After the period of domestic insurrection known as the Northern and Southern Courts Period (1336–1392), the process in which Japan entered the Muromachi Period can be viewed entirely along the same lines.[2] In particular, the Muromachi

[2] This section draws on Hall and Toyoda (1977).

Bakufu based itself in Kyoto, the same as the *ritsuryō* government, and from the onset lacked centralized authority as a nationwide government. The shogun himself immediately became a member of the aristocracy, and the *shōen* and *ritsuryō* systems safely survived with no damage whatsoever. Quite the opposite, these systems were treated as the only ones that were useable. However, it was during this era that provincial powers became even more prominent than they were in prior eras. Directly connected to the shogunate were the *shugo*, and they formed a master–vassal relationship with the warrior class in their appointed province, where they gradually intruded upon the *shōen* in the same manner as the *jitō* in previous eras. This is how a provincial system based on *shugo* domains developed, and the *shugo* came to be known as *shugo-daimyō*. However, these *daimyō* differed from those of the Sengoku and Edo Periods, and in the end it is difficult to say that they formed territories. In other words, they were *shugo-daimyō* as long as they controlled land on the *shōen* level, and because they did not deny the existence of the *ritsuryō* system. As a control type, it occupied the final place in this category.

Accordingly, in the sense that relatively central authority, including military force, conspicuously weakened and made the arrival of a state of anarchy even easier, the control of the Muromachi shogunate was transitory in character, but it is not as though it created the system that would actively support the following era. As we will see in the next chapter, the Muromachi shogunate was unable to effectively grasp the transition to an agricultural village society and economic society.

2.17 Summary of Chapter Two

Japan originally formed a state under the influence of ancient China, and naturally it incorporated the system of the Sui and Tang empires and made up the so-called *ritsuryō* state. Land was placed under public ownership, and the *ritsuryō* state attempted to implement the *handen* allocation system for the purposes of uniform taxation, neither of which became established. Furthermore, from the strong desire for private land ownership by the temples, shrines, and aristocrats, and the relative weakness of the monarchy, which was unable to curb these desires, a land system called the *shōen* system, which was entirely at odds with public seigneur's right, was created. However, this did not mean the abolishment of the *ritsuryō* system; on the contrary, a combination of these two systems became the framework.

The creation of a warrior government in and of itself also did not signify a shift to a new framework, and infiltrated the old framework, but the establishment of *zaichiryōshu* (local seigneur) control, which was unlike the parasitic *shōen* seigneurs, became the link to the next era.

In the economy under the *shōen* system, the seigneurs assumed the *nengu* collection rights held by the ancient state, and the in-kind *nengu* collected from the peasants was directly consumed, so the formation of markets was extremely limited. The production goals of the peasants were also limited to compulsory items – self-sufficiency and *nengu* – so there were no active attempts to encourage production, and there were no technological improvements. Economic incentives were not at work. Even for the seigneurs, under conditions where territories were not formed and ownership rights were stratified, there was no interest whatsoever in agricultural production or the condition of the peasants, so no attempts at all were made to improve and increase production.

Chapter 3
The Delayed Formation Process of Economic Society

3.1 After the Collapse of the *Ritsuryō-Shōen* System

Based on what we saw in the previous chapter, it is virtually impossible for social fluctuation to occur from within. In particular, it is only natural to question how it is possible for an economic society to form from such an unstable society. However, political instability had the opposite effect of subverting the union between robust political and economic control (the possession of wealth), and as a condition eased the formation of economic society. In fact, had Japan built up its organization as an ancient state with a higher degree of perfection and completed framework of stable control, there is no doubt that Japan's later historical developments would have been somewhat different. Had there been the concentration of authority unique to the typical ancient state, namely a concentration of authority that extended to both the sacred and secular realms, or in both politics and economics, the social framework would have become extremely stable. Yet, although Japan incorporated the framework from ancient China, universal religion entered at the same time, and aided by topographical conditions where several regions formed by being geographically divided, that framework's original compatibility with the ancient state did not become established as is. Nonetheless, as the only framework the Japanese knew, it lasted until the sixteenth century with all of its instabilities, and to the point that it is possible to view Japan as having experienced the ancient state. However, aside from the time when the *ritsuryō* system established itself, this type of ancient state framework was by no means a powerful presence, and it is also a fact that its fate was to eventually collapse internally. Rather, we should be amazed that this fragile framework managed to maintain itself for close to a thousand years.

The problem is what comes after this internal collapse. A situation where there is nothing to take its place is conceivable. This was the case in a majority of East

A. Hayami, *Japan's Industrious Revolution*, Studies in Economic History,
DOI 10.1007/978-4-431-55142-3_3

Asian regions, where there was no new social framework, culture, or value system to rise from the rubble of the mighty ancient states until quite recently. Precisely because nothing could be created, these regions had to bear the hardships of colonization (or semi-colonization) by the European powers. Of course, this was possible in Japan as well, but one of the reasons this did not happen was that Japan was the farthest away from Europe and resource-poor, and more than that, as an internal condition, a “state” based on a single value system was built after experiencing a period of instability prior to the arrival of the Western European powers after the Industrial Revolution. Furthermore, since this state formation was conditioned by the coming of an economic society, it also made it possible to transplant the technological fruits of the Industrial Revolution from Western Europe. One may certainly question the importance of industrialization by reference to its by-product that was harmful to human beings. However, what the author is attempting here is simply to account for the fact that Japan did industrialize, regardless of its consequences.

In this regard, the building up of economic society and the new control system based on it seem to be the central issues.

3.2 Formation of Economic Society in Japan

We start with the conclusion that the formation of economic society began in the areas around the Kinai Plain between the fifteenth and sixteenth centuries and spread nationwide during the seventeenth century. Therefore, during this period Japan experienced a great deal of regional disparity. As far as the period prior to the establishment of unified government, the same can be said for its political aspects as well. The combination of these two shows that local structures during this period were extremely complex.

The first change that resulted in a shift toward creating an economic society occurred within the *shōen* system – the payment of *shōen nengu* with currency instead of goods (*daisennō*). This had already appeared at the end of the Kamakura Period but made significant headway between the late fourteenth and fifteenth centuries. Why were *nengu* originally paid with products now changed so as to be paid with currency? This is likely because it became difficult to transport products as *nengu* during this period. The governing powers of the *ritsuryō* government – an essential prerequisite to the peaceful transport of goods – decisively weakened, and the *shōen* seigneurs were now losing the ability necessary to acquire *nengu* due to invasions by local forces. The amount of the *nengu* to be collected naturally dropped, and during the Muromachi Period, some *shōen* seigneurs who became unable to maintain their urban lifestyles left the capital and spread out across the countryside, forcing them to lower their standard of living. The only remaining means at their disposal was to take the *nengu* in a form that was easier to transport. Currency was the form chosen.

3.3 The Sufficiency of Currency

However, there were many obstacles to replacing the *nengu* with currency. First, there were insufficient currency (or precious metal) reserves. Also, the ordinary peasantry (who bore the burden of paying the *nengu*) was completely disconnected from the circulation of currency. Furthermore, when the *nengu* was received as currency, naturally it had to be converted to everyday essentials, but there were no stores of these either. Therefore, the conversion of *shōen nengu* to monetary payments did not occur all at once, and made only gradual progress as it worked to resolve these issues over an extended period of time.

The first problem is how currency was created. As minted currency, there were already the so-called *kōchō jūnisen* (the twelve types of imperial coins) minted from the beginning of the *ritsuryō* government until the late Heian Period, and gold and silver were in circulation as "currencies by weight," but in the end these were insufficient. Then, the large-scale importation of Chinese currency began. This was the importation of Song and Ming dynasty coins, and large quantities of these were imported from the late Kamakura Period by the *wakō* pirates and trade ships travelling to Ming China. Then, the commencement of this type of large-scale trade during the Muromachi Period politically created a scramble for trading privileges surrounding its profits, and economically caused the creation of a trader/merchant class, trade ports, and trade cities. Of course, importing required exporting. Examples of Japanese exports at that time included weapons (particularly Japanese swords), lacquerware, and sulfur.

The second problem is how the peasantry acquired currency. At first, the conversion of *nengu* to monetary payments probably did not mean that the peasantry immediately turned their *nengu* obligations into cash. Third parties – likely merchants with currency – served as *nengu* collection agents for the seigneurs. In these cases, this meant that the peasants paid their *nengu* in the form of goods, which the merchants turned into currency with the cash they had on hand. The merchants were now required to sell the *nengu* as products.

3.4 The Rise of Markets

The final problem relates to the adequacy of essential items through markets. When urban dwelling seigneurs received the *nengu* in cash, they expended it to purchase daily essentials – in other words, they fulfilled their needs via markets. Cities were no longer populations of consumers in the self-sufficient system between the proprietors and the peasants as they formerly were under the *shōen*, but instead morphed into population centers which served an economic function where money was expended to purchase necessary items. Here, farming villages surrounding the urban center likely received the greatest impact. Then, as monetization of the *nengu* progressed, its influence expanded, so peasants in these areas were brought into the currency circulation system, and they were then able to pay the *nengu* themselves in cash. Peasants began producing to sell – at the very least that type of production objective brought about a major change in the nature of the relationship with production, in addition to the original objectives of paying *nengu*, and self-sufficiency.

This shows that the conversion of *nengu* to monetary payments had a far greater impact on all segments of society than previously thought, although there are several major caveats. Once again, these changes took place gradually over a period of one or two centuries, and even if *nengu* payments were converted to cash, collecting the *nengu* itself was becoming increasingly difficult. Even taking Kyoto as an example, the population and scale of the city instead went into a decline, and the lifestyle of the seigneurial class, as is often told, also became impoverished. On the other hand, however, a new type of city was being born. Also, the residents of Kyoto – aside from the *shōen* proprietors and its parasitic classes – were forming merchant and artisan classes which dealt in daily necessities. This background can be used to explain the formation of the townpeople (*machishū*) during this period.

3.5 Changes in Rural Villages and Agricultural Production

Now, a look at the influence these changes had on farming villages: Agriculture which provided fresh food was already present in the immediate vicinity of the cities, but at this time the circulation of currency and production for sale rippled out to the urban periphery. Production goals were originally limited, but the addition of the element of "selling" resulted in the easing of the quantity and technology conditions holding back production. Peasants increased their production amounts in some way, and sold the surplus to acquire currency. Also, the introduction of currency into their lives had a number of consequences.

First, how was increased production possible? The first thing that comes to mind is the expansion of arable acreage. This could be made possible without requiring any changes to the original production system. However, in the plains of the Kinai area, the development of arable land proceeded from a very early stage, and there was not much uncultivated land that could be developed with the technology of the time. Consequently, increases in production with these methods would have been slim – if at all – and certainly would have immediately hit a wall. The next thing to come to mind is increasing production within a defined area of arable land. Naturally, this means an increase in land productivity and improved land use. Nevertheless, this was a change that was difficult to achieve with existing production methods and organization. This is because the conventional production organization relied on the utilization of servant labor, and with this type of labor force land use will inevitably be extensive. Particularly in agriculture, concentrated management of labor is difficult, and in tasks where a great portion of production process depends on the individual attitudes of the laborers, large-scale labor mobilization and highly consistent work are difficult to implement with this type of labor force. Besides the force of the whip, there probably were no means to build up labor, and this had its limits in agriculture. The shift in management from servant labor to family management (including that labor force being converted into manager families) appeared as a production-side response to the need for increased production.

However, this conversion certainly was not able to occur easily. For the *myōshu* who customarily managed their lands for generations using *nago* and *ge'nin*, to suddenly share management with several small families was a kind of adventure. This probably also only gradually progressed over a long period of time. First, blood families divided, and after quite a bit of time had passed, the management system using *nago* and *ge'nin* was dismantled. (There are virtually no materials on this issue from this period available, leaving no recourse other than making speculations from materials that record similar facts that occurred in the Edo Period; but see Hayami 1973).

Through this process, the peasant society gradually diffused. This likely began in the areas surrounding cities such as Kyoto and Nara, and some cities such as Sakai and Hyōgo joined midway and spread throughout the Kinai Plain area in the sixteenth century. Management by small peasants became a general phenomenon as a response to increased production, but its influence appeared in variety of aspects. First, agricultural technology set the direction of developments in labor concentration and increased yields per cultivated acre. Since then, the technological demands accompanying irrigated wet rice agriculture, on the one hand, and the historical significance of "family labor", on the other, conditioned the development of agricultural technology in Japan. In other words, the progress has until recently been made largely in the direction of enhancing land productivity, which means that yields per cultivated acre had already reached global standards in the Edo Period.

Second, since these fields were now managed by married couples, and the independent farmers were liberated from their servant status, the marriage rate increased, along with the birth rate. As a result, there was an increase in population. This development will be discussed later, using examples from the Edo Period.

Third, deeper horizontal links between peasants accompanying the spread of their own management style cannot be ignored. Under the *shōen* system, the word "peasant" (*hyakushō*) could have a very broad meaning, and included several strata of society that had disparate interests – from the *myōshu* down to the *fudai* and *ge'nin* classes. However, when small farmer management spread, this meant that the peasants had common interests, at least as managers. What was created from these circumstances were community organizations with territorial connections called *sō*, *gō*, and *jige*. The fact that these organizations began in the Kinai and its surrounding area during the Muromachi Period and gradually fanned out to the periphery is a noteworthy phenomenon. The peasants now reached the point where they had an autonomous organization in which they shared responsibilities, duties, and rights in accordance with an agreement (Tonomura 1992). These types of organizations would likely not have formed had only a handful of large-scale *myōshu* managed a village, or among them several layers with disparate interests had existed.

3.6 Economic Incentives

The transition to peasantry management accompanied the changes in production objectives, namely, the inclusion of production for the purposes of selling. Moreover, regardless of whether land was owned, the peasantry became a presence where they were responsible for managing land, with married families as the basic unit. Of course, this does not mean that they were completely free to choose the crops they would grow or when they would do it. Use of common lands, use of water, and certain agricultural tasks had to follow community order. However, this gave the peasants who were able to seize economic opportunities the possibility of increasing their income in the form of cash. It must be noted that a feature of cash is the ability to accumulate it and exchange it for necessary commodities at any time. For example, the peasants were also able to purchase land with a certain amount of cash. In the beginning, even the "independent" peasants who did not hold land were given this chance.

The introduction of economic incentives to peasant life brought about great changes to their daily lives and thinking. Their thinking toward production changed as well. Labor went from being a response to an unavoidable burden to becoming a "virtue" which had the promise of greater economic income and a higher standard of living. As a result, they were able to bear its physical hardships. Family labor was the labor force best suited to this. Since families doubled as managers, hard work and long hours were a type of investment that could result in future rewards.

However, the permeation of economic objectives and money into the lives of the peasants did not bring about only economic development. Just as there were those who seized opportunities, there were also those who failed and were ruined. Money in particular tormented the peasants in many cases due to the heavy burden of debt. The peasant uprisings that swept across the Kinai Plain region in the early fifteenth century had a deep relationship with the formation of autonomous peasant unions described earlier, but the fact that the primary focus of their attacks was the moneylenders shows that this was a response by a peasantry incorporated into the monetary system.

3.7 Changes in Urban Areas

Along with these changes in farming villages, there were also changes in urban areas such as Kyoto and Nara which brought about functional changes, and in addition, a new type of urban center whose original existence was premised on its denizens engaging in economic activity (such as the port towns Sakai and Hyogo). Then, as production-for-sale permeated society, a chain reaction occurred where commodities were collected and distributed in logistically convenient areas, such as along waterways and highways, resulting in the creation of new market towns where merchants and artisans resided. Places such as Imai in Yamato, which even to this day retains a visage of those days, are towns that were born during this period. Then, the product distribution net that linked these cites covered the entire Kinai Plain.

However, these changes cannot be overly simplified. From the Ōnin War (1467–1477) on, the Kinai area was frequently ravaged by warfare, and at its center was Kyoto, which also fell into a conspicuous decline. It was no better outside of the Kinai area, where the situation remained for the most part unchanged. Aside from a few exceptions, cities had no development, and farming villages retained old forms of agricultural technology and organization, and for a large majority of these peasants, money was something completely unknown. Consequently, production standards were also low, and a great distance still lay between them and the creation of economic society. Therefore, it is safe to say that regional economic disparities during this period were extremely large. Production-for-sale was carried out in the Kinai Plain region, currency circulated, the people behaved economically, and economic value became its foundation. Agriculture was performed in a manner different from that of other regions, and intensive small-scale management expanded. Groups of people with autonomous organization were formed, and several cities in particular were well-known as "autonomous cities." These cities were autonomous to the point that they even looked like European "autonomous cities" to the Europeans who arrived at the end of the sixteenth century. However, it is necessary to recall that the creation of these "autonomous cities" as a peculiar presence in Japanese history was possible under the state of political anarchy that existed at the time. Once unified governments formed, these "autonomous cities" were brought under their jurisdiction with practically no resistance.

3.8 Sengoku *Daimyō*

Compared to the formation of economic society in the advanced regions in the Kinai region, what were conditions in the outlying areas like? In Kinai, in contrast to the economic changes, nothing new was created politically. Far from it, this region was the final stronghold for both the *shōen* owners and the Ashikaga shogunate, and was the last area where the *shōen* system remained. In the outlying areas, on the other hand, the control of both the *ritsuryō* system and the *shōen* system became virtually non-existent between the Muromachi and Sengoku Periods, and a form of anarchy existed. However, from this, through competition via forces in the local seigneurial class, regional authority grew. Normally, these people are called the overlord of a warring state (*sengoku daimyō*).

The overlord of a warring state who survived the turbulence of the Sengoku Period until its very end were the Date, Gohōjō, Imagawa, Takeda, and Uesugi in the east, and the Chōsokabe, Mōri, Nabeshima, and Shimazu, et al. in the west, and they created a sphere of influence that spanned a number of provinces over several generations. Clearly, these *daimyō* had their base in the peripheral provinces, and were not connected to the aforementioned economically advanced Kinai area. However, their controlling structure was something new in the sense that it no longer had any substantial relationship to the *ritsuryō* system, the *shōen* system, the Muromachi shogunate, and the *shugo daimyō* system.

Basically, the overlord of a warring state established loyalty relationships while recognizing the local seigneuries originally held by the small-scale local seigneurial class as *honryō ando* (shogunate recognition of land-holding rights in exchange for a pledge of loyalty), and broadened their sphere of power. Of course, along with territorial expansion, the connection to the land weakened, and in the areas directly controlled by the *daimyō* (known as *kurairichi*) a system was adopted where a *daikan* (an official representing the *daimyō*) was in control, but strong local control became the governing principle. Most of the retainers lived in the villages performing agricultural cultivation, and the warriors and farmers had yet to be separated, so later development into a castle town (*jōkamachi*) was also either nonexistent, or on a small scale.

However, had a lord–vassal pyramid hierarchy formed in this manner, it might have been worthy of the name "feudal." The reason is that under this system the most important thing was that the retainers' lower-level lordships were recognized. A status quo was maintained where retainers with military force resided in the farming villages and exercised territorial control over a fixed expanse, which included the management of directly controlled lands.

As the *daimyō* power sphere expanded, in the end a form of state order became necessary. Their relationships with their retainers also were inevitably unstable, as they recognized lower land lordships (in fact, how many revolts occurred during this period!) Here, it was a series of legislation known as the *kahō* (overlord of a warring state family code) and the *bunkokuhō* (domain law) that gave a legal character to these relationships.

Surprisingly little is known about the relationships between the lords and peasants under the overlord of a warring state system. One form was *honryō ando,* where existing relationships continued, and in actuality there was no systematic unity. However, when previous relationships were destroyed via military conquest, it was necessary to establish a new relationship.

The overlord of a warring state completed the formation of their territories by eliminating the existence of any control rights other than those belonging to them or to their retainers, but at the same time, it was necessary to enrich their territories and strengthen their armies, so they had to manage their possessions well. The resources they needed were not merely prowess as military generals – like those when the Kamakura shogunate was founded – but also administrative skill in order to maintain stability in their territories. From this need, the overlord of a warring state put considerable effort into creating conditions for production within their territories. The best-known example is the river flood control projects and mine development in Kai Province by the Takeda. The Kasumi-*tutumi* – the embankment constructed to prevent floods along the Fuefuki and Kamanashi rivers in the Kōfu Basin which used a series of discontinuous levees with a forest serving as a flood break – still function effectively to this very day. These fairly large-scale improvements in production conditions carried out by the *sengoku* lords can be viewed as having created increases in production and stability, seeing as how these types of projects had been interrupted for a very long time (from the beginning of the *ritsuryō* system). Here, there were increases in production through methods different from that in the advanced areas in Kinai. Next, what is important is that under these circumstances the peasants' *nengu* obligations also possessed the character of a public tax, not a private rent like the *shōen nengu*. A qualitative evaluation of the *nengu*, not just its amount, must be added.

However, the overlord of a warring state control structure had a major weakness. This weakness did not manifest itself as fighting among the *daimyō* themselves, but as will be described later, it became a decisive weakness when it clashed with a force with a different control structure. After all is said and done, the overlord of a warring state were from economically backward areas which did not experience what had already occurred in the Kinai area: general circulation of currency and changes in production organization. Agricultural production still took a form that included a reliance on servant labor. The situation where there was no division of labor between warriors and farmers was also an inescapable fetter as long as it was premised on this type of agricultural production. The reason is that if this division were forced, agricultural production would be destroyed. Also, the fact that there were strong ties to the land served as a brake against territorial expansion and the *daimyō* themselves advancing into the central areas. A situation like that of the Edo Period, where lords were separated from the land and the *daimyō* were forcibly relocated to other domains, was inconceivable.

However, these weaknesses were indeed the characteristics of "feudalism." Even in Western Europe, the feudal system was created on the premise of lax economic activity, and in Japan, when the overlord of a warring state system is measured in European terms, it can be said to most closely resemble the feudal system.

3.9 Regional Disparities

Thus, Japan during the Sengoku Period assumed a form where a combination of political and economic developments mutually intersected atop a regional structure: although the Kinai region economically advanced, politically old forms remained, and in the periphery, while politically a separate seigneur system (most closely resembling feudalism) developed, it was politically behind. Therefore, in order to unify Japan under these circumstances, a control structure that combined both regions under a unified principle was required, and the fact that this task was undertaken by rulers who came from an area between these two regions – Oda Nobunaga, Toyotomi Hideyoshi, and Tokugawa Ieyasu – originated from Mino, Owari and Mikawa Provinces, all grown from the Eastern Central area, cannot be dismissed as a coincidence.

During the latter half of the sixteenth century, the overlord of a warring state completed their territorial expansion in the peripheral areas, and just as they were targeting the center, a new model of ownership, based particularly in the region surrounding the Kinai area and the Nōbi district (Mino and Owari provinces), developed. Oda Nobunaga's power structure differed from that of other overlord of a warring state: "warrior–farmers" were separated into warriors and farmers, group drills were performed using entirely standing armies, and although they were few in number, they possessed formidable military force. Just at this time, firearms were introduced to Japan through contact with the Portuguese (more on this below), and it was a weapon well suited to this type of military organization. The Nōbi district, owing to its location in the Kinai periphery, made gradual changes during this period due to the infiltration of the transition to the new economic society being developed in the Kinai Plain area. As a result of the form of agricultural production changing into that of small-farm management and increases in production, the lords were able to take the drastic step of carrying out military reforms where warrior–farmers would be separated into dedicated professions. On the one hand, this resulted in the creation of consumer populations in the form of castle towns, which also stimulated the farming villages, and encouraged the shift to economic society. In contrast to the Kinai region, it was to this region's advantage that it was never subsumed under any of the former powers, which meant that the new lords did not have to pay any heed to existing control systems.

Under this of new lordship system, their military power had the advantage in its clashes with the overlord of a warring state. Oda Nobunaga's successor, Toyotomi Hideyoshi, completed unification of the country in a relatively short period of time. This lordship system was created in places where conditions made it possible to spread small-farm management, circulate currency, and separate warriors and farmers into separate professions. However, in the process of national conquest, this spread beyond the region in which it was created and spread nationwide. In other words, through replacing the *daimyō*, between the end of the sixteenth century and the beginning of the seventeenth century, the overlord of a warring state were forcibly relocated to other provinces (with very few exceptions), and lords were forced to lose their ties to their own land. This was made possible through the adoption of the *kenchi* (nationwide cadastral survey) and *kokudaka* (tax assessment system based on the amount of rice produced) systems, which will be examined later. In this regard, this meant that the supreme authority – be it Toyotomi Hideyoshi, Tokugawa Ieyasu, or the shogun that followed – possessed great authority over the *daimyō*. In extreme terms, the *daimyō* had no idea when they would be ordered to transfer to another province on the shogun's whim. The retainers were also severed from the land. Most of them settled in the castle towns, and even if they were allotted territory in the form of *jikata chigyō* (fiefdom assignments), lordships came with restrictions. In other words, normally their rights were limited to a fixed percentage of *nengu*, but they were prohibited from placing the peasants in their territory into a state of servitude or collecting anything other than official *nengu*, and they had no legal jurisdiction over the peasants. Therefore, it was possible to switch over to a stipend system at any time.

It is difficult to understand this form of control using the term "feudal" as is, and it is due to these circumstances that phrases like *shūkenteki hōkensei* (centralized feudalism) and *kaitaiki hōkensei* (dissolution-period feudalism during the Edo Period) have been used. Therefore, in Japan, if measured using European history as a yardstick, the period that most closely resembles the "feudal system" was relatively short, and in a limited area. Also, what followed was an ownership system that took the form of control premised on conditions where there was a certain degree of economic development, which included the separation of warriors and farmers, and the formation of cities. Before discussing this, we shall first touch upon the fluctuations in the international environment that occurred at about that time in and around Japan.

3.10 International Environment

During the sixteenth and seventeenth centuries, the international environment surrounding Japan was busy. Combined with the simultaneously progressing domestic changes, it was a very turbulent era for international relations, and ultimately, Japan chose *sakoku* – a condition to reduce foreign relations to a minimum. When thinking about the Edo Period, the fact that Japan entered a period of *sakoku* became the element that politically, economically, and culturally defined that period, so it is necessary to have a complete grasp of foreign relations during this period.

Already from the beginning of the Muromachi Period, the brave warriors along the coastline in northwestern Kyushu piloted small boats to strike at the Korean Peninsula and continental China and commit acts of piracy. They were the so-called *wakō* (Japanese pirates). They were not necessarily all Japanese, but the presence of these pirates can be explained by the military vacuum in these regions. The Ming Chinese and Korean governments were unable to manage the situation and frequently requested that the Muromachi shogunate suppress these pirates, but the shogunate was powerless to stop them, and in the end, foreign relations between Japan and these countries even broke down as a result.

Also the Ryukyu Kingdom enjoyed its golden age in the East China Sea trade as an intermediate merchant, between China, Korea, and Japan.

If these pirates are viewed as Japanese expansion overseas, then Japan's advancements into Southeast Asia could be viewed as a continuation of this. Between the late sixteenth century and early seventeenth century, there were many merchants who set out to trade with China, the Indochina Peninsula, Siam, Malaya, Indonesia, and the Philippines, and Japanese towns were formed in some of these areas and there were even some Japanese who became mercenaries for foreign armies. Toyotomi Hideyoshi and the Tokugawa shogunate issued "vermillion seal licenses" to authorize trade in an attempt to regulate it and use it as source of revenue, ushering in the era of the so-called vermillion-seal ships.

Thus, Japan's foreign relations, which were formerly almost virtually passive in nature, completely changed character during this period, although short, and a proactive shift was made from Japan to overseas. This was a result of changes that occurred in the mutual, relative positions due to the decline of the powerful presence of ancient empires in the Korean Peninsula and continental China, which peaked with the fall of the Sui and Tang empires, and Japan finally establishing itself as an independent power. Also, this momentum became Hideyoshi's reckless expedition to the Korean Peninsula after he completed the unification of Japan, but due to that failure, and followed by the implementation of the *sakoku* policy, Japan's short-lived foreign relations once again contracted inward.

Another major experience in foreign affairs was contact with European powers and Christian culture. At first, the nation of Portugal and the Jesuits, a Christian missionary organization, monopolized relations for a while, but at the end of the sixteenth century, the nation of Spain and the Franciscan and Dominican monastic groups joined, and in the seventeenth century, the Dutch and English approached Japan and drove out the Catholic nations. During the *sakoku* period, among the European powers the Dutch East India Company's monopoly over trade with Japan was complete. Understanding the rapid changes during this short period, and the process leading to *sakoku*, requires us to shift our focus toward an explanation of Portuguese and Spanish expansion overseas.

Portugal, which had deep ties with Japan in the late sixteenth century, is today regarded as not a powerful nation in the European Union, but in the fifteenth and sixteenth centuries Portugal, along with Spain, actively expanded overseas. Regarding Africa and Asia, Portugal opened up the sea lanes around the Cape of Good Hope, established colonies, and monopolized trade. This overseas expansion should be understood as an extension of the Reconquista, which has a long history on the Iberian Peninsula. In this region, Christianity spread from the latter days of the Roman Empire to the period of tribal migration and the era of the Visigoth Kingdom, but the Visigoths fell to Islamic invaders during the early eighth century, and the entire Mediterranean seacoast came under the Islamic sphere of influence. A movement to reclaim the Holy Land arose in the eleventh century, and Crusader armies were sent numerous times. Part of this was a movement to also take back former Christian lands on the Iberian Peninsula from the infidels. This was the Reconquista. This movement occurred over the space of several centuries over the entire Iberian Peninsula, and at the end of the fifteenth century, Islamic forces were finally driven out. Portugal was a Christian nation born of this process and was founded in the twelfth century. It used its power to work its way south, and successfully ventured to the western coast of the African continent from the thirteenth century onward.

On the other hand, the Byzantine Empire, a bulwark of stability in the eastern Mediterranean, collapsed, and the trade connecting east and west became unstable. For Europeans, spices, particularly black pepper, was an essential seasoning for meat, so the interruption of trade with the Moluccas Islands – the source of black pepper – had great significance. In addition, from the fourteenth century onward, as a part of Renaissance thinking, the notion that the earth was a sphere was asserted, so routes leading to the East which took a southerly route (via the Cape of Good Hope) or a westerly route (a western journey across the Atlantic Ocean) started to be considered. At the time, issues related to the Protestant Reformation and various domestic issues in Western Europe remained unresolved, so both of the monarchies on the Iberian Peninsula, which also jutted out in a southwestern direction geographically, decided to bring about quick unification, inherit the long-distance navigational techniques formerly controlled by Islamic culture, and support these adventures.

Portugal and Spain divided their areas of expansion through the Treaty of Tordesillas, under which Portugal was the one that primarily went into Asia. The Portuguese fleet rounded the Cape of Good Hope in 1497 and arrived in India, seized control of the Indian Ocean within the space of just a little more than ten years, and then arrived in the Moluccas Islands, where pepper was produced. During that time, they established several outposts, which they fortified in order to monopolize Asian trade. Traded items were loaded on ships bound for Lisbon, and from there these products were introduced into European markets via Antwerp. Wealth flowed into the monarchy, ushering in a time of prosperity.

However, these advances by the Portuguese into East Asia inseparably linked trade and Roman Catholic missionary efforts. Originally, the motives for this advance were trade and missionary, and the monarchy was the point linking the two. The reason for this can be found in the historical background of these two Iberian countries. In extreme terms they were societies that consisted of the two monarchies, the aristocracy surrounding them, and poor peasants. There was almost no middle class, and in economic activity in particular, there was virtually no place for commoners to become involved. Therefore, a resulting characteristic is that although this may not have been the case when the monarchy had a monopoly on trade, once competitors appeared these weaknesses were immediately exposed.

Nonetheless, the reason that East Asian trade was monopolized by this nation with insignificant military forces was a result of the divided nature of the Asian countries of the time. For example, India, the first society the Portuguese arrived in, was divided into several small local domains, and was unstable due to the strife between Islam and Hinduism, so Portuguese colonial outposts (Goa, etc.) were established with ease. For Portugal – a nation with a small population – concentrating its trade and missionary activities in these colonial outposts and linking them via naval power was its sole means of expansion.

Now, Portugal – which dominated the East Asian spice trade – had no need for further expansion, and made some minor contacts with southern China to request trade. Places like Japan were not included in their objectives at all. Therefore, relations with Japan commenced by an accident after close to half a century had elapsed since Portugal's advances into East Asia. It is said that Portuguese contact with Japan commenced one day in the 1540s when a Chinese junk with some Portuguese on board were shipwrecked on Tanegashima Island. Yet, once relations with Japan began, Japan was seen as a prime target for trade and proselytization.

First, regarding trade, in Japan, which was in the middle of the strife of the Sengoku era, in particular, in the Kyushu region, which first had relations with Portugal, the regional powers sought to enrich their provinces and strengthen their soldiers, so new weapons (particularly firearms) became hotly sought-after commodities, and from economic gains due to trade, the various *daimyō* gladly welcomed the arrival of Portuguese ships in their domains. In addition, under circumstances where central government existed in name only, there were no governmental bodies to check foreign relations.

In the area of proselytization as well, the climate in Japan was also more hospitable compared to the other areas the missionaries visited on their way from Portugal, and the natural conditions were suited to proselytization activity requiring transmission of teachings over a long term. In addition, religious activity in opposition to the Christian missionaries was not very strong in Japan, unlike India and Southeast Asia. Naturally, at the popular level, the highly influential Nichiren and Jōdo Shinshū sects of Buddhism engaged in proselytization, but this was also virtually limited to central Japan and did not extend out toward western Japan. The commoners had a latent desire to seek spiritual peace amidst these endless revolts, and in western Japan, Christianization made rapid headway in the late sixteenth century. The Jesuits established churches, monasteries, hospitals, and colleges, so Japan experienced a "Christian century" (see a modern classic, Boxer 1951).

Another point to be made regarding trade is that it was evident that trade with Japan was highly profitable. In Japan at that time the comparative price difference between gold and silver was almost 12:1 (gold:silver), making silver in Ming China much more expensive. However, due to the termination of relations between Japan and Ming China, the two countries did not seem to be aware of this difference. The Portuguese, as a foreign third-party intermediary, were able to reap enormous profits. They exported silver from Japan, changed it into gold in China, which they then brought back to Japan and exchanged for silver. Even a casual calculation will show how much profit could be gained from these exchanges, which also did not require very much by way of expenses. For these reasons, trade and proselytization both became key objectives in Japan, and Macao increased in importance as a base of operations. Recent studies have shown that silver exports from Japan accounted for about one-third of the world's silver production at the time (approximately 40–50 tons) of peak at the end of the sixteenth century. Also, this trade became a valuable source for the funds Portugal required to manage its East Asian operations and the Jesuits required for proselytization.

At first, Japan was completely excluded from Portugal's objectives, but around the same time Japan started to be noticed as an objective, Portugal's status went into a rapid decline. In the 1580s, the King of Spain created a situation where he was able to hold both the Spanish and Portuguese crowns for over half a century due to a royal succession issue. Spain supported Magellan's voyage around the globe, which then led to its already possessing the Philippines as a colony in the 1520s. Dominican and Franciscan monasteries headquartered in Manila began to proselytize in Japan. At the same time, domestic unification made headway in Japan, and Toyotomi Hideyoshi in particular harbored suspicions toward Christianity, so these proselytization competitions by these sects were extremely negative overall. Each sect slandered the other to Hideyoshi, ultimately leading to a period of trial for Christians in Japan: the expulsion, persecution, arrest, and execution of missionaries. Hideyoshi learned from his previous expeditions to Kyushu that the city of Nagasaki had been donated to the Jesuits, so he ordered them to return it, and issued an order expelling the missionaries. However, trade was especially heavily weighted for Hideyoshi's finances, so although he prohibited missionary activity, he was unable to ban trade, therefore his foreign policy was unstable. Although he issued the order expelling the missionaries, sometimes he met with missionaries and their emissaries at Osaka Castle and permitted proselytization. However, in the end, as a domestic unifier, a single, unified ideology became necessary, which was something incompatible with Christianity. For the Tokugawa clan, land had great weight in its finances, so it was much easier to sacrifice trade; and since Confucianism was clearly made the ideology, Christianity gradually became the target of persecution. Finally, the so-called *sakoku* order was enacted, using the Shimabara and Amakusa rebellions in the 1630s as an excuse, leading to a policy of total oppression.

On the other hand, among the European nations, Spain also plummeted in influence due to the defeat of the Spanish Armada in 1588. Spain was not able to prevent England and Holland – countries that finally got their domestic affairs in order – from attempting to expand overseas. Japan also commenced relations with the Dutch when their ships arrived in 1600, and then the English. At this point, competition with the two Iberian nations for trade commenced. England and Holland had separation of church and state, and since trade was carried out by the East India Company – an organization of merchants that received privileges from the government – this was a much more suitable relationship for the Tokugawa shogunate. At first, an East India Company commercial house was erected in Hirado, followed by one in Nagasaki on orders from the Tokugawa shogunate. Portuguese royal trade, which rested atop a monopoly, had no choice but to retreat in the face of this more efficient style of commerce, where branch offices were opened in major cities. However, due to the British East India Company's failure to acquire Chinese articles for import to Japan, such as raw silk, and because sales of English products were not good, in addition to the company's trading area being restricted to Hirado and Nagasaki from 1616 on, they finally closed down their commercial houses in 1623, after a mere decade. Afterward, they decided to concentrate their business efforts in India. Also, the Portuguese, who were unable to separate trade from proselytization, and had also become militarily inferior, were finally banished from trading with Japan in 1639 after close to a century of doing business there, and Holland was the only country remaining as a result. Here, with the monopolization of the Nagasaki trade by the Dutch East India Company (trade with Chinese junks was also allowed), from the Japanese standpoint, *sakoku* was complete.[1]

How can this type of *sakoku* be assessed? Thus far, primarily the negative aspects have been emphasized. Due to the loss of contact with the outside world – in particular, prohibiting Japanese from travelling abroad or returning to Japan – overseas expansion that was gaining in activity suddenly dropping to zero was a major loss, both culturally and economically. Markets were limited to domestic ones and even served as a laboratory for a closed economy in Edo Period Japan. Recently, in contrast, there are also views that observe an opposite meaning, claiming that the energy that had been focused outward was now focused inward due to *sakoku*, resulting in the Edo Period's being a time of extremely sophisticated culture. In economic

[1] However as a result of recent studies on foreign relations in this period *sakoku* is considered a misleading word. Particularly in the Tokugawa Period, the use of *sakoku* is misleading. See Toby (1984).

history, at least during the early Edo Period, domestic markets had room to expand, and market constriction due to *sakoku* did not seem to be at work, but in the latter half of the Edo Period, it should be assumed that economic development was blocked by limits.

However, what we want to call attention here is not the influence of *sakoku* itself, but the evaluation of the fact that *sakoku* could be carried out. The negative evaluation of *sakoku* is likely the right one, but thus far no consideration has been given to the government's decision to carry out *sakoku*, or the fact that it was able to do so. (At least in the beginning, there was no sense of *sakoku* in Japan, so it may be more accurate to describe it as "a result, a series of diplomatic measures that came to be known as *sakoku*".) The notion that *sakoku* was negative is nothing more than our modern assessment based on our knowledge of later developments in world history. However, whether Japan was able to carry out *sakoku* or not was its sole ability of the time. In this first contact between East and West, naturally the East Asian countries responded in various ways. Yet, the majority of them would have been unable to implement *sakoku* even if they had wanted to. The countries between Southeast Asia and the Indian subcontinent were relegated to colonization until second contact was made after the Industrial Revolution.

Therefore, the choice of *sakoku* (meaning "closed country") of Japan – and its execution – is evidence that Japan engaged in a form of state-building at the time. That is why it was likewise possible for Japan to perform a 180-degree policy turn, open the country, and be the first among the East Asian nations to industrialize over 200 years later, although there were many problems. This is of course not to say that we should ignore the fact that the historical developments in the closed system while *sakoku* was in effect were in the direction of accepting the technologies and systems of modern society brought forth as a result of industrialization. However, consideration of the common roots which made the diametrically opposed choices of both *sakoku* and opening the nation possible should also not be dismissed.

One more thing that could be said from a general survey of the international relations of this period is the matter of its very delicate timing. If the domestic unification of Japan had been several decades later, it is unmistakable that the posture Japan could have taken would likely have been very different when Christianity and Dutch and English ships arrived. Or, it is possible that *sakoku* would have been entirely impossible. Also, the competition among the European powers was a drastic change. At the most drastic point in the developments of both histories, both made contact and produced that kind of result.

Finally, however, there are several conditions that must be kept in mind regarding the description above. First is that the conditions associated with the word *sakoku* are quite distant from reality. A window was open via Nagasaki, and foreigners came to Nagasaki (although in extremely limited numbers) and even travelled as far Edo. Japanese people also learned of world affairs entering through Nagasaki. Trade in Nagasaki was managed by the shogunate, and although the quantities and items did not have the definitive influence on the national economy as it did from the Meiji Period onward, as we will see in the next chapter, there were several major processes that cannot be ignored. Not only in Nagasaki, trade with Korea by the

Tsushima Domain (*han*), and trade with the Ryukyus by the Satsuma Domain were officially authorized, and according to recent research, it is clear that there was a period when the amount of that trade far surpassed the trade at Nagasaki. Furthermore, if the trade with the Ezo, and unrecorded illicit trade are also taken into consideration, it is a mistake to look at *sakoku* in strict terms. It is also not as though there were no Japanese who traveled overseas. Near Busan, in Korea, there was the *Waegwan* (Japanese quarter) where diplomacy and trade were carried out. Overseas knowledge entered Japan in the form of *rangaku* (Dutch Studies), of which fields such as medicine, natural science, and art were particularly conspicuous, and these had a great impact on the formation of rational thought.

Also, it is a mistake to seek the causes of *sakoku* solely on the Japanese side. Regarding silver and copper, Japan was one of a handful of countries around the world that exported it. Conflicts among European nations regarding their acquisition had a predilection toward monopolies as a type of mercantile trade, and *sakoku* must be looked at from this type of global historical background.

3.11 Summary of Chapter Three: A Great Transition

The conversion of *shōen nengu* into monetary payments was the impetus for currency being used in the everyday lives of urban denizens, and necessities were satisfied through markets. This had an impact on the farming villages in Kinai, and aside from the existing objectives of self-sufficiency and *nengu*, the peasants began to incorporate elements of sales into their production objectives. The introduction of economic incentives changed peasants' attitudes toward production, and changes to a more efficient form of production began. This was the spread of minor farmer management. On the other hand, a new type of cities or towns such as trading cities and market towns were created which primarily performed economic functions, and in the Kinai Plain economic society came into being. In order to fill the void in seigneur control, autonomous residents' organizations developed in the cities and farming villages.

On the other hand, peripheral areas were economically backward, and the overlord of a warring state who severed their ties to the *shōen* and *ritsuryō* systems created feudalistic land ownership control, and territorial formation could be seen, and seigneurs started to implement measures to increase production.

Then, finally, Nobunaga, Hideyoshi and Ieyasu, who were from intermediate areas that possessed the strengths of both systems, completed unification. These lords on the one hand stood atop conditions where economic society spread, and carried out the separation between warriors and farmers and the formation of castle towns, controlled their retainers and peasants based on the *kokudaka* system, and created a new framework to replace the *shōen* and *ritsuryō* systems.

International relations also made great changes at the same time as these domestic political and economic developments. First, the Japanese (who had been entirely passive up to that point) started to expand overseas and migrated in large numbers to areas in Southeast Asia. Also, Japan commenced contact with the European and Christian powers they had virtually no relationship with up to that point. In trade and proselytization, Portugal had close ties with Japan. However, governance of foreign affairs began along with the rise and fall of the European powers between the sixteenth and seventeenth centuries and domestic unification in Japan and, in particular, Christian proselytization were incompatible with the ideology of the unifiers, which led to the 180-degree turn known as *sakoku*. However, the fact that Japan was able to choose *sakoku* and implement it could also be viewed as evidence of a form of state formation.

Chapter 4
The Establishment of Economic Society and the Edo Period

4.1 The *Bakuhan* System

As stated in the previous chapter, the government established by quelling the anarchy of the sixteenth century had its foundations in regions where small-scale management in agriculture had already spread with the permeation of economic society and increases in production were becoming a reality; it was premised on the progression of the separation of warriors and farmers, as well as warriors, merchants, and artisans residing in urban areas. In the advanced regions in Kinai and its surrounding areas, the fact that the economic society that formed took precedence, and seizing control of such areas was by no means the same as seizing control of other areas which had not experienced the change toward economic society yet.

Toyotomi Hideyoshi and Tokugawa Ieyasu actively forced the *daimyō* to relocate to other domains. The *daimyō* from advanced regions were required to gain experience as lords in backward regions, and the overlord of a warring state were also forcibly estranged from their land. Also, the *kokudaka* – the average production amount assessed through the cadastral surveys known as *kenchi* – became the sole standard, and its amount determined the pecking order for the warriors from the *daimyō* on down. Therefore, during this period the *daimyō* were lords[1] with land values expressed in "tens of thousands of *koku*" – the volume of rice production – and they were not the owners of *specific* lands. The same held true for the *daimyō*'s retainers. A *daimyō* with 200,000 *koku* was a *daimyō* with the rank of 200,000 *koku*, and it did not matter where he possessed his land as long as its value was 200,000 *koku*. Thus, the nationwide political system was called the *bakufu-han* (*bakuhan*) system.

At the same time, *kokudaka* also became the standard for taxing the peasants, in reality not directly but through the village, i.e., *muradaka* (*kokudaka* of a village). During the Edo Period, villages were officially responsible for *nengu* obligations.

[1] After the collapse of *shōen* system, the term "lord" is used instead of "seigneur" in this volume.

A. Hayami, *Japan's Industrious Revolution*, Studies in Economic History,
DOI 10.1007/978-4-431-55142-3_4

However, for example, a village having a rice crop yield of 1,000 *koku* meant that the value of the land converted into an amount of rice was 1,000 *koku* of this village and the levy was determined by either the *kemidori* (where the yield was assessed annually) or *jōmendori* (where the *nengu* was a fixed rate based on the average yield over a period of several years) method based on the village's rice crop yield. Therefore, the *kokudaka* system is what characterizes the *bakuhan* system, and since it was the cadastral surveys that made it possible, we shall now look at these surveys from that viewpoint.

4.2 Initial Cadastral Surveys

If taken literally, cadastral surveys are the classification of land and the measurement of its surface area, but the large-scale surveys carried out by Toyotomi Hideyoshi (commonly known as *taikō kenchi*) or those carried out when the *bakuhan* system was created (including the *taikō kenchi*) have great significance as the basic operation that enabled a control structure based on the new *kokudaka* system.[2]

It was Hideyoshi who placed great stock in the cadastral surveys and expanded them nationwide, but even in his case, remaining records show that they initially assumed the form of the *sashidashi* reports (cadastral surveys based on documents submitted by villages). Here, village leaders were required to submit reports regarding the village's land, production yields, and its original *nengu* amount, so the methods for measuring production yields were woefully inadequate. Along with the transition toward minor farmer management, there were quantitative and qualitative changes in production in Kinai and the surrounding area, making it impossible to continue the *nengu* and production yields as is under the *shōen* system. Therefore, Hideyoshi took the next step and initiated *jōryō kenchi* (measuring cadastral surveys) based on overall land surveys and the finalization of average production yields for each grade. Then, he appointed his trusted subordinates as *kenchi bugyō* (cadastral survey inspectors) and dispatched them to lands that were conquered militarily or yielded to Hideyoshi via negotiations, and these magistrates conducted cadastral surveys nationwide. According to the diary of one of Hideyoshi's confidants, at Osaka Castle Hideyoshi learned through the accumulation of cadastral registers (*kenchichō*) as a result of the cadastral surveys that the lands he could use freely increased, so he was satisfied.

Defined systemically and narrowly, Hideyoshi's large-scale cadastral surveys were the surveys whereby Hideyoshi issued orders, appointed magistrates, promulgated the ordinances related to the cadastral surveys, and conducted them in each province regardless of lordship. However, the *taikō* land survey in this narrow sense was not implemented nationwide. A fair number of cadastral surveys were performed by the local *daimyō* on their own land in accordance with Hideyoshi's wishes. In

[2] The section draws on Hayami (2009).

these cases, there was no problem when the person performing the survey was one of Hideyoshi's direct retainers or a lord of similar standing, but problems occurred when the *daimyō* was of a different character – such as a overlord of a warring state. For example, in the case of the cadastral survey performed by the Chōsokabe clan in Tosa Province, the content of the cadastral registers used as historical source material (actually, they are called *chikenchō*) and their recordation methods are quite different. As the Chōsokabe had yet to separate the warriors and farmers in their domain, they recognized the subordinate lordship of their retainers, so compared to cadastral registers in which only the name of a single peasant was recorded for a tract of land for areas where this was not the case, the recordation method they were required to adopt was complex.[3] Therefore, in these cases, consideration must be paid to the character of the *daimyō* performing the cadastral surveys. Henceforth, the surveys performed by *daimyō* of equal standing as Hideyoshi, combined with the *taikō* surveys in the narrow sense, will be called "initial cadastral surveys." There were some exceptions, but as a result of the surveys performed by Hideyoshi, the nationwide *kokudaka* in 1596 was calculated to be over 18 million *koku*.

As a result of *kokudaka* estimates due to the initial cadastral surveys, the *daimyō* and their retainers were positioned using the *kokudaka* as the standard, making it possible to extract *nengu* from the villages. The *daimyō* had tables listing the estimated village *kokudaka* at their disposal, so based on these, they were able to determine the location of the land they would grant to their retainer that corresponded to their defined *kokudaka*. Thus, the retainers existed apart from their land and became a bureaucratic cadre residing in the castle towns.

On the other hand, another role performed by the cadastral surveys was that the "village" became the *nengu* assessment unit and administrative unit due to the fact that the surveys were performed at the village level (in some cases, towns). In this case, "village" roughly corresponds to present-day *ōaza* (subdivisions in rural municipalities), and at the same time, it signified communities as a unit of daily life in rural villages. As a result of the overlap between villages as administrative units and villages as living units, village communities already formed under names such as *sō*, *gō* and *jige* were given a robust framework.

Daimyō who conducted the initial cadastral surveys knew from experience that tracts of land managed by small farmers had high yields, so they could expect even greater amounts of *nengu*. Moreover, even taken from the general principle that the subordinate *daimyō* of the retainers was not recognized, denying the existence of junior lordship among the peasants meant political stability as well. Then, laws known as the so-called small farmer autonomy policies were issued. The text of these laws clearly denied compulsory service among the peasantry and collection of tenant rents, and stated that the person paying *nengu* should be the person actually cultivating the land. This makes the intentions of the *daimyō* evident. Incidentally, there is a complete lack of historical materials that speak to how these laws were implemented or what types of penalties were imposed when they were violated.

---

[3] In Taikō's cadastral survey, the name of a peasant was recorded at the bottom on the form, with one name to one plot of land. But in the Chōsokabe survey, double or triple names were recorded.

Also, an earlier viewpoint positioned the cadastral surveys as a measure to realize these autonomy policies, but this view is negated for the following two reasons.

It illogically links the cadastral surveys and minor farmer autonomy policies and is based on the fact that the names of the peasants recorded in the cadastral registers signify the owners or cultivators of the land and at the same time were the ones responsible for making *nengu* payments. However, since the *nengu* was assessed at the "village" level under the *bakuhan* system, it was unnecessary for the *daimyō* to establish individual land holding. Also, if the cadastral surveys served to establish peasant land holding, it is difficult to comprehend why the Meiji government had to establish individual land holding when it revised the land taxation system. For these two reasons, it is evident that the cadastral surveys certainly did not extend to land holding by individual peasants. However, the fact remains that the names of peasants were written in the cadastral register, and the assumption that the village bears ultimate responsibility was merely a formality, so in the end, someone had to share this responsibility. However, this is already beyond the scope of the cadastral survey and cadastral registers. How *nengu* assessments were divided within a village can be confirmed by historical documents produced by the village (normally called *nayosechō* where the holders' names are listed). The names listed in the cadastral registers and *nayosechō* ledgers did not necessarily overlap (generally, more names appeared in the cadastral registers than the *nayosechō* ledgers). It is known that prior to the end of the seventeenth century there was a considerable gap between the two. This accurately testifies to the fact that the purpose of the initial cadastral surveys was not to confirm or establish the land-holding rights of individual peasants in the cadastral registers. Therefore, the initial cadastral surveys were not a method for creating legal autonomy for individual farmers.

If this is the case, it cannot be said that there was no relationship whatsoever between small farmer autonomy policies and the initial cadastral surveys. The implementers of the initial cadastral surveys laid the foundation for their own authority above "minor farmer autonomy." So, for each piece of land the names of the peasants (certified holders of the land known as *nauke'nin*) were simply listed in their cadastral registers. In other words, this ledger format shows that there was no intervention whatsoever by those who possessed junior lordships between the land holder or cultivator and the *daimyō*. In contrast, as revealed earlier, the case of cadastral registers of the overlord of a warring state had two or three written columns, showing that a complex lordship relation was acknowledged as is. Also, for the cadastral surveys performed by the Tokugawa themselves, which were strongly compromising in nature, there were the so-called *bunzuke kisai* (double registrations), and the junior lords and cultivator holders were doubly written in two columns. This was previously understood as an indication of the regional character of the backward areas, but this interpretation cannot be used to explain the fact that joint registrations are not seen in the cadastral registers Hideyoshi prepared for Mutsu and Dewa Provinces of the northernmost area, but are seen in the ones that Ieyasu prepared for the Kantō and Shinshū regions, near central Japan. Rather than saying this is a regional matter, perhaps we ought to say that it is a matter of the character of the person implementing the cadastral survey. Perhaps the Tokugawa, who were originally from Mikawa Province, adopted a cadastral survey policy different from that of Hideyoshi (who acquired the economically developed Kinai region), as a result of moving eastward to backward areas such as Shinano, Kai, and the Kantō region.

Thus, the initial cadastral surveys were a survey of *land*, and not one of *land holding*. The objective of the initial cadastral surveys was to investigate the types, location, and amount of land and how much land was held by the villages as a taxation unit.

4.3 The *Kokudaka* and *Murauke Nengu* Systems

The *kokudaka* system enabled through these cadastral surveys and the *murauke nengu* (village contract) system are the most important supports which systemically characterize *bakuhan* society. The *daimyō* were able to use production yields assessed through the cadastral surveys as a taxation guideline. It was far more efficient compared to taxation under the *shōen* system, and was able to at least partially get a handle on the shift to new production. Yet, in actuality the *kokudaka* system was rigid in several aspects and was flawed in its inability to adapt to change. In particular, due to its connection to the social order in *bakuhan* society, and the maintenance of the *bakuhan* system itself was postulated on this order, the *kokudaka* system faced the contradiction of having to treat production yields – which are variable by nature – as a fixed value. Of course, we deem this a contradiction based on modern-day judgment, since we know that as an early-modern society the Edo Period was one where there were stunning increases in production, but the people at the time probably felt no contradiction whatsoever. Specifically, the *kokudaka* system was rigid in the following ways. Namely, whether a *daimyō* or a retainer, the social rank accompanying one's household was determined entirely by *kokudaka*, making it a standard that had to be maintained. Of course, a political mishap could result in a decrease or elimination of one's *kokudaka*, or conversely, meritorious deeds could result in an increase. However, during the tranquil days of the Edo Period, these types of changes did not occur very frequently. In particular, major changes happened on extremely rare occasions. Therefore, for example, a "300,000 *koku daimyō*" meant that he was assessed 300,000 *koku* during the initial cadastral surveys, but even if he increased 200,000 *koku* more on productivity of his territory, he was not allowed to perform another survey and become a "500,000 *koku daimyō*." New cadastral surveys were performed internally and have been called *naiken*, but even these were unable to keep pace with increased production. At most, *daimyō* were able to perform cadastral surveys only on newly developed land. Even here, the only thing they could do to encourage new land development was to assess the land using loose standards. Thus, the numerical yields allotted to the *daimyō*, villages, and peasants gradually diverged from actual production levels. Moreover production increases by no means occurred uniformly nationwide, so these allotted yields gradually lost their significance as an index. When analyzing *bakuhan* society, *kokudaka* are often used since they are a convenient number at first glance, but excessive reliance on them as an economic index must be avoided.

4.4 Economic Structure

We shall now examine the economic structure under the *bakuhan* system in its entirety from several angles. Figure 4.1 shows the flow of assets and currency among various social components and the reader is asked to compare it to the one for the *shōen* system (Fig. 2.1).

Figure 4.1 makes the following clear: (1) the circulation of currency and assets included all three of the classes shown here; (2) the *nengu* the lord took from the peasants was definitely a non-economic behavior, but considering the existence flowed from the opposite direction, we should find at least a portion of the *nengu* was returned to the peasants (or the merchants and artisans as well) as governmental expenses or social capital paid by the lord– in other words, the *nengu* was not purely a private rent, but also possessed the characteristics of a tax.

In addition, the *nengu* was standardized into two forms: currency and rice, and the lord converted most of the *nengu* received as rice into currency by selling to the merchants, which they used to purchase daily essentials. Therefore, it is possible to establish the *nengu* as a form of indirect consumption. Under this form, the lord

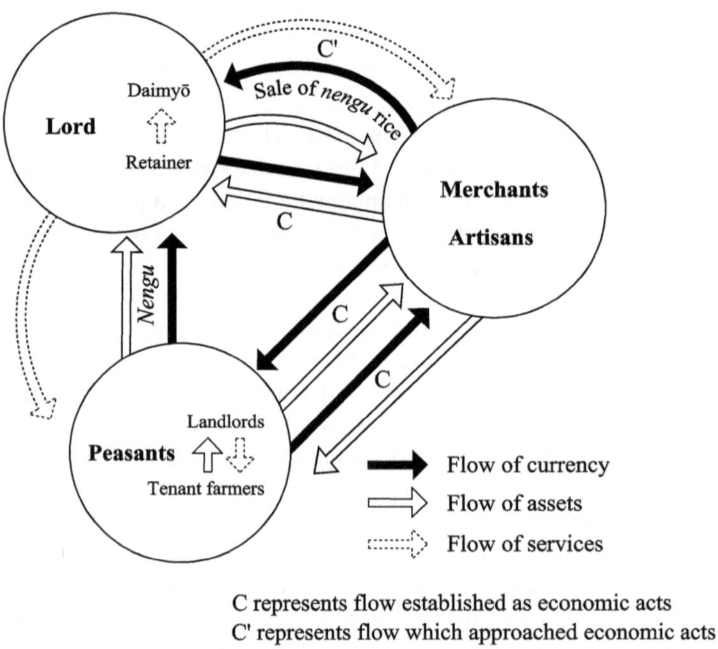

Fig. 4.1 The Flows of Goods and Currency in the Early Modern period

class had to perform the behavior of selling the *nengu* rice, but the matter of whether the nature of this behavior is economic or non-economic is a subtle one. For the shogunate, at first the payout value of the *nengu* rice was determined at their initiative, primarily balancing it with their finances. This is the so-called *oharigami nedan* (fixed price label) system. However, among the rice transacted in the market, when the rice that the merchants directly purchased from the peasants (also known as *nayamai*, or rice stored in a peasant's barn) increased – not *nengu* rice (also known as *kuramai*, or rice stored in official warehouses) – it gradually became difficult for the shogunate to unilaterally determine the *oharigami nedan* price from the standpoint of its finances; so conversely, the actual market transaction price took the initiative. As a system, the *oharigami nedan* lingered for quite some time, but substantially this came to possess the character of an economic act.

Also, when the lord class purchased goods from the merchants as consumers, in many cases it was a commercial behavior. However, the lords frequently exercised their privileged samurai status in their financial dealings and failed to repay their debts, or the government issued orders cancelling debts. However, over the long term this also was by no means a unilateral victory for the lord class, as the merchants received special privileges, participation in the finances of lords, and the right to make statements in exchange.

All acts among the merchants, or between the merchants and peasants, were economic behavior, and what ultimately remained until the very end was the behavior of the lord taking *nengu* from the peasantry. The Meiji Restoration was the abolition of this act and the land tax reform implemented immediately after. Moreover, when the *nengu* was taken as a percentage of the production yield, it was at a surprisingly low level. When the land tax reforms were enacted, the *nengu* was 30% in government surveys as well, and in actuality, it was probably much lower.

Thus, the circulation of currency and assets meant that all strata of society had the potential to seize economic opportunity and enrich themselves. However, in actuality, the samurai class was virtually unable to seize these types of opportunities. They became increasingly impoverished. This was particularly conspicuous among the lower-ranking samurai, but not a single higher-ranking samurai created assets during this period. (Bear in mind that wealthy persons from samurai origins all created their wealth as a result of their activities after the Meiji Restoration.) The fact that the samurai class, which had political power and control rights as lords, could not attain any kind of wealth, and the fact that the abolition of control rights as a lord class in Japan differed from the French Revolution in that it was almost bloodless are truly major historical characteristics. These characteristics are powerful evidence that in Japan political and economic power were alienated from one another, and that control rights as a lord were not built on such a strong foundation (connection to land).

In contrast, the merchants, artisans, and peasants were in a position where they could seize economic opportunities. The fact in and of itself that these politically controlled classes accumulated wealth and gave rise to a wealthy class is a characteristic of this period of Japanese history, and is by no means a universal phenomenon that occurred globally. Thus, a society where commoners engaged in economic activity, creating economic winners and losers thorough competition – which were not present during the ancient and medieval epochs – was precisely the basis on which the Edo Period can be called "early modern." Forgetting the meaning of that type of historical training it experienced, and just painting broad strokes over this period as one of exploitation and poverty is not an accurate assessment.

4.5 Economic Change during the Edo Period

In short in the Edo Period economic activity was opened to masses, and with this as foundation, popular culture (in particular, townsman (*chōnin*) culture) flourished during this era. With the exception of those residing in the immediate vicinity of urban areas, for peasants during the Muromachi Period and earlier, undoubtedly knowing absolutely nothing about currency their entire lives, during the Edo Period, as will be discussed later, agriculture was an occupation that required capital investments, and even the poorest peasant could not survive without a connection to money. Along with the matter of what was brought about as a result, we must first think about the meaning of these types of changes.

First, the following three indicators make it clear the degree to which the Edo Period was one of intense economic change. The first is the population, which is believed to have increased more than threefold during this period. In other words, the population showed a change from approximately 10 million people (±1 million) to 33 million. Originally, the initial nationwide population was said to be 18 million, but there is no scientific foundation for this. Rather, based on estimates made by the author of the present work, the population was far less than that, and there is a strong possibility that the aforementioned numbers are correct. Therefore, the nationwide population increase was greater than originally thought.

Next is the amount of cultivated acreage, which increased by approximately two-fold. The basis for this is that when the *taikō* cadastral surveys were completed in 1598, there were 1.8 million *chō* (17,850 million km^2) of cultivated acreage, and during the early Meiji Period, there were 4.4 million *chō* (43,634 million km^2) of cultivated fields. However, it can be assumed that the surveys performed during the *taikō* surveys were incomplete, so between these two a two-fold increase would likely be a reasonable interpretation.

The third is the production yield (*kokudaka*), and this indicator is the one with the greatest number of problems. First, the nature of *kokudaka* was by no means one of production yield; rather, the most approximate expression would be to say that it was the overall value of the agricultural goods produced converted into rice volume. However, the conversion rate was nothing more than the surface area of the field multiplied by an expected yield (*kokumori*). At any rate, this was 18 million *koku* under the *taikō* surveys. What would have happened had the survey been performed during the early Meiji years using the same standard? There is great room even for debate regarding the production statistics of the early Meiji years, but rice was at approximately 40 million *koku*, and cereals were at approximately 10 million *koku*. Of course, aside from these, crops for food and industrial raw materials were cultivated. It is extremely difficult to convert these, but taking population increases and living standard increases into consideration, it is not unreasonable to consider increases that are at least four-fold. Moreover, considering that among the population the proportion of the non-agricultural population increased even more, the increase in agricultural production may have been even greater.

These kinds of increases in the economic indicators (of course, they are the values of nationwide totals, and naturally they include regional disparities and disparities within time periods during the Edo Period) were of a size entirely inconceivable during prior eras. Take population for example. During the approximately 300 years of the Edo Period, the 3.3-fold increase means that during the period the population continuously increased at an average rate of 0.4% a year (in actuality, as will be explained later, there was a rapid increase during the first half, followed by conditions close to stagnation, to once again shift toward an increase at the end of the Edo Period). Had these conditions continued for 500 years, the population would have increased by a factor of eight. Therefore, projecting backwards the population in 1600 was 10 million people. This means that in the year 1100 it would have been 1.2 million people, and in the year 600 it would have been 150,000 people. This is entirely unrealistic. Based on the remaining family registers, the nationwide population during the Nara Period (eighth century) is estimated at approximately 5.6 million people. In other words, population increases commenced somewhere not too far from the beginning of the Edo Period, and prior to that there were either no long-term increases, or even if there were, they were insignificant. The fact that economic fluctuations during the Edo Period (increases in various elements) were this intense is not that unexpected when viewed from prior assessments of this period. This is because the fluctuations after the full-scale commencement of industrialization were even more intense, so the fact that there were major fluctuations in the period directly before was concealed.

Incidentally, the three aforementioned indicators all show the intensity of the changes during this period, but when viewed in their respective combinations, the proportions between them also changed. The greatest increase was in *kokudaka* (production yield), followed by population, with the increases in cultivated acreage being the lowest. Therefore, the production yield per unit of cultivated acreage increased, but the cultivated acreage per capita decreased. Also, production yields per capita increased somewhat.

The conspicuous increase in yield per acre signifies the development of intensive agriculture. On the other hand, since production yield is a value that is extremely difficult to ascertain, it is also possible to view this degree of increase in per-capita yields as being within the margin of error. However, among agricultural products, the production yield mentioned here is that of foodstuffs (particularly grains), and when other forms of agricultural production are added, it is likely that it rose even further. Among the population, the increase in the agricultural population was certainly lower than that of the increase in the overall population based on the conspicuous increase in the non-agricultural population, or the urban population. Therefore, it is quite conceivable that peasant per-capita production yields increased to a certain degree.

This final peasant per-capita production increase will likely be an extremely important factor when taking preparations for industrialization into consideration. This also suggests that if distribution is not skewed, or if it is slightly skewed, there is the potential for the living standards of ordinary people to improve. Actually, the living standard of the peasants during this period should be seen as having improved. Even the poorest peasants no longer lived in crude hovels with earthen floors. They started to wear clothing made of cotton, use ceramic utensils, and consumed a considerable amount of animal protein (from fish meat). Demographic indicators – particularly increased average life expectancies – more than anything reflected improvements in living standards and living conditions in the period before advancements were made in preventative medicine and public hygiene. Put into extreme terms, during prior eras, the servant labor provided by the *fudai* and *ge'nin* were treated practically like livestock;they were not allowed to form families and they were complemented primarily by the members of higher-ranking peasant families who did not have the opportunity to serve as successors to their families. However, during the Edo Period, although they were servants, there was a fixed term of service, they received a salary, and they were treated as human beings. Of course, compared to the present, they were mired in poverty and lacked modern freedoms. However, be that as it may, depicting the lives of the people during this period in excessively gloomy terms only serves to cover up the importance of this era.

4.6 Economic Spheres

Here, we will examine the economic spheres of the Edo Period. During this period, the formation of markets advanced on several levels, but the fact that an economic sphere covering the entire nation formed atop the economic spheres covering regions (or domains) is worthy of attention. In other words, this type of phenomenon did not exist prior to the Edo Period and served as a major premise toward industrialization.

The shogunate was based in Edo, which in and of itself meant that Edo was able to become a city supporting a considerable population, but in addition, through the adoption of the alternate attendance system (*sankin kōtai*), Edo became a city home to the *daimyō* from all over the nation, as well as their families and retainers. There were some individual differences, but it is said that the *daimyō* spent roughly one-third of their *nengu* income on expenses related to living in Edo and travelling between Edo and their home province. Adding the expenditures made by the shogunate itself, and the *hatamoto* (the shogun's enfeoffed bannermen), among others, it is safe to say that over half of the expenditures by the lord class were made in Edo. Moreover, the lord limited the *nengu* payments to rice and currency, and made additional expenditures upon converting the rice to currency. In other words, with the exception of rice, all daily essentials were obtained via markets. Therefore, even just the population of, and consumption by, the warrior class alone was enormous, and in addition, the consumption amount of the merchants and artisans who formed residential communities synergistically attracted a large population here. The total population is said to have reached one million people during the mid-Edo Period. Conceivably, Edo may have been the world's most populated city at that time. No matter how low the standard of living was, the quantity of daily essentials such as food, fuel, clothing, and building materials consumed by an urban population of one million was considerable. This era was one where transportation methods – particularly land transport – were very poor, and the collection and supply of such a large amount of products was likely a major problem.

When Edo was first founded, the Kantō district was still a backward area, almost no goods supplying Edo's huge market were produced, and even monetary currency had not spread among the common people. Naturally, there were no changes to the production technologies that had already been developed in the Kinai plains areas, with no organizational changes nor any increases in production ability. It was there that the city of Edo was suddenly born, which rapidly increased the consumption amount. Nearby farming villages were undoubtedly influenced by this, but their ability to supply goods and resources was limited. Also, in Edo's early days, the flood control measures along the Tonegawa and Arakawa rivers, which flowed through the Kantō Plain, were insufficient, so production was unstable.

Naturally, for much of its necessities Edo heavily relied on the Kinai area, which had a high level of supply capacity and developed cities, so Osaka assumed significant importance as a supplying depot. Moreover, Osaka was more than merely a material collection and distribution center for the Kinai area, it was also the terminus for the sea shipping lanes through the Seto Inland Sea, which were of definitive importance in the days of sailboat shipping. By using these sea lanes to connect all of western Japan, as well as the Japan Sea coast sea routes, the Kinai area was connected to the San'in Hokuriku and Mutsu/Dewa regions, and even Hokkaido (the Ezo territories). It may seem strange that the products from Mutsu/Dewa and Hokkaido passed through the Sea of Japan and the Seto Inland Sea (the western sea route (*nishi mawari*)), and through Osaka, but this was because the shipping lanes directly connecting these regions and Edo (the eastern sea route (*higashi mawari*)) were extremely perilous in the area south of Shiogama/Ishinomaki down to the Bōsō Peninsula, so navigation was difficult. This was because there were no suitable ports of call along the way, in addition to the unfavorable winds and currents. During the days of sailboats, the existence of ports of call were absolutely necessary, made all the more so by the fact that Japanese-style sailboats in particular lacked a center board, so it was impossible to sail against the wind. The Japan Sea coast could be navigated on most days, excluding the winter months, and ports of call were appropriately spaced apart. It was much easier to navigate. Light cargo was offloaded at Tsuruga and Obama in Wakasa Bay, and then made its way to the north shore of Lake Biwa, where it was sent to Kyoto and Osaka by land carriage. However, for heavy cargo, or large volumes of cargo, ships went all the way down to Shimonoseki, since it was difficult to transfer the cargo for overland shipment.

Thus, Osaka became a national economic hub where products from all over the country were collected, except for those from the Osaka–Edo route, the Kantō area, and its surroundings. As such, the economic activities of the Osaka merchants – for whom the entire country was one large market – were remarkable to the point that it is carried on by modern-day "Osaka merchants." These activities reached their peak during the Genroku Period (1688–1704), which gave birth to a literature – by Ihara Saikaku and Chikamatsu Monzaemon, for instance – and even formed a unique culture. On the other hand, Edo was the terminus for nationwide product distribution and was in a geographic location where a majority of products had to be shipped via Osaka.

In this sense, merchandise transactions between Osaka and Edo were the main arteries of the Edo Period economy. The majority of products flowed in the direction of Osaka to Edo, which gave rise to two professional shippers. Naturally, there were products that flowed in the opposite direction, such as *hoshika* (dried sardines) produced in Kantō for consumption in Kansai, but their overall quantities were not so large. All varieties of foodstuffs, seasonings, luxury items (in particular, *sake-alcohol*), clothing and the materials for clothing (particularly cotton products), fuel, oil, building materials, and all other bulk daily essentials were transported.

Naturally, it can be assumed that currency flowed in the direction opposite that of the products. However, this currency flow was additionally offset by the flow of currency in the reciprocal direction, so in actuality, it is not as though large quantities of cash were constantly being transported between Edo and Osaka. Then, why was a stream of currency moving in the opposite direction (in other words, from Osaka to Edo) created? This was the money the shogunate and *daimyō* earned by selling the *nengu* rice in the Osaka market. At the beginning of the Edo Period, the circulation of currency was almost entirely limited to the Kinai area, and merchants who could target nationwide markets were not found outside of Kyoto and Osaka, so the shogunate and *daimyō* built warehouses in Osaka, transported the *nengu* rice to them, and converted it to currency. Then a considerable portion of the currency was sent to Edo, where it was used for necessary expenses. Therefore, the flow of currency from Edo to Osaka was handled by the merchants, and the flow of currency from Osaka to Edo was handled by the lord class. However, this caught the attention of professional moneychangers (something akin to a modern-day banks), who established branch offices in both Osaka and Edo and commenced transporting money between the two areas. Using this system, the lords could deposit the money they received for *nengu* rice to the Kansai branch, and receive it at the one in Edo. Also, the Edo merchants sending payment for commodities to Osaka submitted their payments to the Edo branch, and payments could be drawn from the Osaka branch. By doing this, merchants were liberated from the dangers of sending money, and currency settlements were handled between the branch offices of these financiers. The Mitsui and Kōnoike were the families responsible for this.

Circumstances between Osaka and the provinces were somewhat different. Opposite the flow of goods from the areas of production to Osaka was the flow of currency from Osaka to the provinces, but this was not offset by the movement of currency between the lords, and ultimately, this was siphoned off by the lord class in the form of *nengu* from the peasants (who were the producers), which was consumed locally or in Edo. At any rate, this created a flow of currency and commodities covering the entire nation.

4.7 The Currency System

During the Edo Period, the ordinary people learned of currency for the first time, and they were greatly affected by incorporating it into their lives. However, the currency system during this period was far more complex compared to the present one. There were three types of currency accepted nationwide: gold, silver, and copper, and there was also *hansatsu* (domain paper currency) as a local currency. Also, the *ei* was used as a nominal unit for calculating *nengu*. These various forms of currency were considered to have value independent of one another, resulting in the creation of an exchange rate. Therefore, in modern terms, the people of this era used several different forms of foreign currency whose rate fluctuated daily. At first, the shogunate established official exchange rates where one *ryō* of gold equaled 50 *momme* of silver, which equaled four *kammon* of copper coin (one *kammon* of *ei*). However, in reality, aside from the latter days of the Edo Period, one *ryō* of gold equaled around 60 *momme* of silver, which equaled around six *kammon* of copper coin, so it could be said that the exchange rate fluctuated at a level of plus or minus 15%. Market rates were created from the fact that the quantity of precious metal contained was a factor determining its trustworthiness, and credit relationships were formed due to the supply and demand for currency. The *bakufu* frequently reissued currency, and most of it was "debased currency" (where there was a reduction in the amount or percentage of precious metal contained) used to resolve fiscal difficulties, so this weakened credit. Throughout the entire Edo Period, the first hundred years were ones of weak inflation, and towards the end of the Period, inflation was rampant.

Gold was on a quaternary notation system (one *ryō* equaling four *bu*, with one *bu* equaling four *shu*), and coinage was minted in the following denominations: *ōban* (ten *ryō*), *koban* (one *ryō*), *nibukin* (two *bu* gold coin), *ichibukin* (one *bu* gold coin), *nishukin* (two *shu* gold coin), and *isshukin* (one *shu* gold coin), among others. Even the smallest unit, the *isshukin* (which in actuality was rarely minted, so the *nishukin* was the *de facto* smallest unit of currency), was worth 1/16 of a *ryō*, making it equivalent to something between 1,000–3,000 yen today, so it was far beyond the reach of everyday lives of the common people. Once we reach the level of the *ōban*, they were almost never transacted in daily business but were used as gifts and had their own exchange rate *vis-à-vis* the *koban*. Using the initial Keichō *koban* as an example, its weight was that of 4.76 *momme* (1 *momme* =3.75 grams), its gold content was 84.3%, or a quantity of 4.0 *momme*. However, for the Tenpo-era *koban*, which was the last coin to be minted in large quantities, its weight was that of 3.0 *momme*, its gold content was 56.8%, or a quantity of 1.7*momme*. The Man'ei *koban*, the last coin to be minted, had a weight of 0.88 *momme*, a gold content of 56.8%, and a gold weight of only 0.5 *momme*. Looking at just the gold weight, it was reduced to approximately one-eighth.

Even if we assume that it was necessary to consider the direct causes – e.g., the solution of the *bakufu* to the financial crisis (as they held monopoly minting rights over gold and silver currency) – for the circulation of this type of debased currency, what is of greater importance is that objectively it was in response to the increase in the amount of circulated currency required for economic development in Japan. Precious metal resources were scarce, but even so, their constant importation was also difficult under the conditions of the *sakoku* isolation – with the major exception of the Tanuma era.

Consequently, aside from the so-called devalued currency, there were no increases in issued currency. During the first half of this period, there was clear correspondence between devalued currency and price inflation, but this became less so during the latter half. This means that as a result of stimulated economic activity, there was great demand for currency. The recasting of coinage which accompanied these exceptional rises in the currency ranking (such as the Kyōhō-era recast) was unpopular because the decrease in the amount of circulated currency that followed the recast brought about financial stringency.

On the other hand, silver was not an engraved currency (one where the currency is defined by the value indicated) like gold, but a weighed currency. Silver clumps of varying shape were weighed on a scale, determining their value. At first glance, this may appear extremely inconvenient, but gold was too exorbitant as a unit for transactions, which made silver convenient for everyday use. However, the content of silver coins also decreased, and what started at 80% pure ended as a mere 13% pure in the silver coins minted during the Ansei era (1850s). The major change in silver currency was the silver coins with their value indicated in gold, known as *nanryō nishugin* or *nanryō isshugin*, which were minted from the Tanuma era onward (1767–1786). This was enacted as part of Tanuma's economic expansion policies, but it also indicates that people of the time were no longer very particular about the type or quantity of precious metals the currency contained.

Also, it is said that gold was used in Kantō and silver in Kansai, but to be accurate, in Kantō the value of goods was indicated in gold (*kinme*) and in silver (*ginme*) in Kansai, and as far as the currency, both gold and silver were used in both regions.

As far as copper coins, *kan'ei tsūhō* (coins minted between the Kan'ei era and the end of the Edo Period) made primarily of a copper-based alloy circulated with a value of one *mon* per coin. With few exceptions, up until the Tempō years the higher unit of currency was a minted 100-*mon* coin, so the majority of engraved currency during this period was irregular, where currency between five-yen coins to 1,000-yen bills (in today's money) did not exist.

The exchange rate for copper coins was low in the cities but high in rural villages (particularly along the highways), and there were also seasonal fluctuations. Moneychangers existed at all levels, and much like in Edo, at least one existed on each street. This is a profession that was born from a complex currency system. Yasuda Zenjirō, who made a fortune in the latter days of the period, took advantage of these fluctuations.

Hansatsu were paper bills issued by the *daimyō* with the consent of the *bakufu*, as opposed to coins, for which the shogunate had monopoly minting rights. In many cases, as a method for solving fiscal difficulties, the *daimyō* stopped the circulation of official currency within the domain, compelling a conversion to *hansatsu*. At first, credit was low, the market sunk, so currency did not circulate well. Ultimately, *hansatsu* made a gradual recovery, and circulated as a type of official currency with a specified premium attached later. In this sense, we probably can consider that it functioned as a means to offset the insufficiency of precious metals compared to currency requirements.

Ei refers to a type of currency known as *eirakusen*, and its exchange rate against copper coins was 4:1, but in reality it is not as though there was a currency displaying *ei*. Gold was assessed on a four-grade scale, and even the *shu*, the smallest unit, was worth quite a bit, so the rate of one *ryō* to one *kan* of *ei* coins was used during *nengu* calculations.

As seen above, a complex currency system which modern people would unlikely be able to readily adapt was the one that ordinary Japanese experienced at first. However, within this system, people were trained in a sense about markets and exchange rates. Also, during this period, currency gradually moved away from its original value based on its precious metal content and became something that circulated based on its face value, resulting in the circulation of low-quality currency. This allowed the government to settle currency without using bullion as a precious metal standard, easing its burden. At the same time, the formation of economic society permeated Japan, although even today conditions in Japan are not such that there is extremely high confidence in precious metals as there is in Western Europe. Also people are not concerned that the government's foreign currency reserves mainly consist of dollars and have relatively little gold. Even if we assume that what is brought about from this is an issue for future study, the fact of the matter is that the manner in which currency was engaged during the Edo Period comprised a historical factor.

Chapter 5
Economic and Social Changes in the Edo Period

5.1 Direction of Technical Development and the Creation of Work Ethics

Agriculture during the Edo Period did not just have several-fold increases in production yields, but there were also major changes in production technology, production organization, in addition to the attitude of peasants to work. These changes had an extremely large impact on the Japanese society and economy, continuing up to the present day.

First, the phenomenon of economic society creation in the rural villages, which started in the Kinai plains and infiltrated the periphery in the sixteenth and seventeenth centuries spread rapidly across the nation as soon as the Edo Period began. This is due to the lords' (with the major exception of the Satsuma Domain) adopting policies to separate the farmers and warriors and mandating the construction of consumer population centers known as castle towns, as well as creating the mega metropolis of Edo, which was followed by the development of Osaka, giving the entire nation the opportunity to produce commodities for selling. Furthermore, the lords were able to enforce monopoly lordship within their domains, also making large-scale flood control projects possible, leading to the stabilization of production in plains areas such as the Kantō Plain. Also after the Osaka battle that destroyed the Toyotomi family, until the middle of the nineteenth century, Japan enjoyed *pax Tokugawa* for more than two hundred years.

Thus, the changes that originally occurred in the Kinai area extended nationwide. Roughly between the years 1700–1750, management dependent on servant labor disappeared, completing the transition to small household management.

Since the factor of "selling" was added to the peasants' production goals, they were motivated to improve production methods in order to increase production or produce goods of higher quality. Naturally, the feasible method was the development of labor-intensive agriculture, which mainly resulted in increased yields per square acre, but it was precisely this active encouragement of peasant production

A. Hayami, *Japan's Industrious Revolution*, Studies in Economic History,
DOI 10.1007/978-4-431-55142-3_5

which, as Japanese industriousness, became one of the major elements which supported industrialization after the Meiji Restoration. Intensive agriculture and family labor were closely linked, in addition, through the channel known as the "family system," and the notion that hard work was a virtue was passed down to future generations.

However, it is dangerous to view these changes in a rosy manner. What is meant by this is that in a material sense, the premise required for industrialization is the creation of a spiral where increased labor productivity is accompanied by improved living standards, the creation of surplus labor, and the preparations for the creation of capital. As stated earlier, the per-capita yield for peasants certainly increased, so clearly there were improvements in living standards, and it appears that this favorable upward spiral existed. However, labor productivity refers to production yields per unit of labor. In modern societies, the value of labor is homogenized via markets, so labor productivity does not take productivity yield per unit of labor (which is difficult to calculate) as its value, but something closely resembling per-capita labor in the working population, or the per-capita production yield. However, this does not work in pre-industrial societies. Labor markets were without a doubt in a process of formation, and this was even more the case for a non-market supply-and-demand system of family labor; labor was not homogenized. In other words, long working hours and severe labor were possible. Therefore, the per-capita production yield becomes too rough a value to be used as a productivity index. We believe that upon entering the Edo Period, the opposite happened: the peasants started to perform hard labor for long hours. Direct observation of this is close to impossible, but we can indirectly learn the following fact: during this era, there was a dramatic decrease in the number of livestock used for agriculture. Livestock are literally "stock" – a production factor in agriculture – and this decrease had to be replaced by another factor. Moreover, since there was an increase in production yield, we can view this decrease as having been complemented by an increase in land production capacity, or an increase in the amount of invested labor.

Looking at the decrease in livestock as an example, in 838 villages in the Mino and Owari regions (Nagoya Domain territory), where comparison is possible, the absolute number of cows and horses decreased by approximately 45%, from 17,825 to 8,104 between the years 1660 and 1810. Moreover, the population increased during this period, so the number of cows and horses per capita decreased by approximately 35%, from 0.055 to 0.019. The greatest decreases were in the Owari plains, and there was a 15% decrease in the Nakashima and Kaitō districts (conversely, there was a 59% decrease in the mountain districts in Mino). Thus, the cows and horses still being used for agriculture in the 1670s were practically no longer in use by 1810. This tells us that for farming, animal labor was replaced by human labor.

When these types of changes are compared to those of Western Europe, which similarly saw an increase in agricultural production yields immediately prior to industrialization, the differences become evident. In Western Europe, increased production yields were carried out primarily through massive injections of animal labor power. By having several – ultimately, as many as twelve – horses pull large, heavy plows, problems with large-scale cultivations and deep plowing were simultaneously resolved. Here, we can say that there was clearly an increase in actual capital, there were savings in per-capita labor, and production yields greatly increased per capita (or per unit of labor). Therefore, a change known as the Agricultural Revolution took place in England (where this tendency was particularly evident), which was then succeeded by the Industrial Revolution.

Incidentally, the reverse happened in Japan – actual labor increased – so despite the fact that the peasants were now behaving economically, the formation of subjects headed toward industrialization and the development of labor-saving technology did not occur on a large scale, to say the least. Even if research is performed on Edo Period farming villages, industrialized subject formation cannot be detected, and nothing more than the conditions were created. It is precisely in this regard that economic history, particularly the progression of industrialization in Japan differed from that of the West.

However, we should take the view that adequate conditions were created. Therefore, once industrialization agents were created due to external impact, there was sufficient capacity for industrialization. In this regard, research from this viewpoint has been omitted from numerous prior studies.

Now, the development of intensive agriculture and the spread of small-family operations shrank the average operational size. Of course, there were regional differences, and we can assume that they would have been able to manage with even smaller tracts of land if they grew off-season crops. However, standard management during the Edo Period considered one hectare of rice fields and half a hectare of vegetable fields to be the agriculturally sustainable land area for households consisting of a married couple and several children.

5.2 The Results of the rise of Intensive Agriculture

Now, the development of land and labor intensive agriculture and the rise of land productivity simultaneously meant an increased need for efforts to maintain soil fertility. In agricultural production, land may last for several years if it is used without taking the maintenance of soil fertility into consideration, but continuous use beyond that is difficult. There are signs that slash-and-burn agriculture – the crudest method of land use – was still being practiced throughout Japan at the beginning of this period, but the degree of land use increased, and continuous yearly use became universal. Moreover, demand for increased yields meant the introduction of large-scale fertilizer use and deep plowing.

Looking at fertilizers, originally they were made by using underbrush or fallen leaves, and human excrement or livestock manure, along with ash to produce compost (which was called *ryokuhi* – or green manure – during the Edo Period). Tilling this into the soil was one of the methods adopted during this period to maintain soil fertility. These methods could be directly obtained through the labor of the peasants themselves, so in that sense, it was self-supplied fertilizer. Therefore, near their homes, or in an area of the village, it was normal to have a hill of cut grass, a forest on the plains, or a grassland area, and these traditional common lands (known as *iriaichi*) were used under a system determined by the village residents. Nevertheless, the following problems occurred: soil fertility could not be sufficiently maintained with just this fertilizer – which meant that the degree of land use increased; also, the fact that these lands themselves were converted into farmland, made the acquisition of this type of fertilizer (particularly underbrush) difficult.

The latter can be explained by the drastic population increases in farming villages. Thus, in both senses the reliance on existing fertilizer sources inevitably dropped. What appeared in its place were fertilizers such as dried sardines, dried herring, and oil dregs, all of which were obtained from markets via merchants – making them "purchased fertilizer" (known as *kimpi* during the Edo Period). The practice of using fish as fertilizer was a type of wisdom created by Japanese peasants, but the increased reliance on purchased fertilizer had a tremendous influence on agriculture in the following two ways.

First is the influence it had on management. Purchased fertilizer was literally bought with currency, so it was now necessary for the peasants to invest capital into their agricultural production. During the age of self-produced fertilizer, the peasants could engage in production even without capital reserves. Nevertheless, when the use of purchased fertilizer was introduced, the peasants had to purchase fertilizer before the harvest. The majority of peasants did not have that kind of capital reserves, so they had to borrow against their harvest or offer their land as collateral for a loan. Fertilizer and grain merchants became involved in the lives of peasants as they were providing them with financing. A constant in agriculture is that harvest yields and produce prices deviate greatly, so it is conceivable that debts could not be repaid. In these cases, the peasants lost their land, and in a worst-case scenario, houses and peasant labor (peasants themselves or their families) would have to be offered as compensation. Also, the need for cash income in order to obtain fertilizer became of great importance, so they were partially compelled to engage in side businesses and cultivate off-season crops. As a result, the labor to obtain self-supplied fertilizer was reduced, but other types of labor in order to obtain the funds to purchase fertilizer were added. Now, agriculture became an occupation requiring capital, and this change was of great significance.

Another change occurred in the technical realm. Purchased fertilizer was fast-acting. Therefore, fertilizer had to constantly be added. However, additional fertilizers ultimately fertilized the area near the surface, which allowed weeds to flourish. Japan's topographical conditions were already well-disposed to the proliferation of weeds, which were enhanced by the addition of fertilizers, so the peasants had to expend a great deal of labor on removing weeds, as well as fertilization. Furthermore, these fertilizers made the soil acidic when administered in large amounts, which negatively impacted harvests. Deep plowing became necessary in a preventative sense as well. Yet, in Japan increasing the number of livestock and using large-scale tools for deep plowing was impossible in light of the expenses and land required for raising livestock, and was inefficient in small-scale operations. Conversely, during the Edo Period agricultural implements were miniaturized into cultivation tools suited to human physical strength – in other words, a shift from plows to spades and hoes was seen. A variety of spades and hoes suited to the soil quality were realized. Then, in a majority of cases, it became possible to plow somewhat deeper than with a small plow pulled by the single horse or ox previously used. (After the Meiji Restoration, short-sole plows pulled by livestock were re-introduced, making even deeper plowing possible.) Plows replaced hoes which primarily relied on human physical strength.

These technological changes all resulted in the intensification of labor. Peasants were no longer a source of servant labor and became able to act as agents in small-scale operations. However, at the same time, they were required to perform many hours of demanding labor. In a manner of speaking, this was a price they had to pay to be liberated from their status as servants. To the eyes of the foreign agronomists who arrived in Japan during the Meiji Period, this looked like impoverishment (Mayet 1893), and the average life span of male adults during the Edo Period appeared to be stalled, unlike women and people in the lower-age ranges, who saw their life expectancies increase.

5.3 Population Increase in the Early Edo Period

As a result of intensive agriculture establishing family management as a general practice, the population exploded. This has already been discussed previously, but in short, formerly a low marriage rate resulted in a low childbirth rate, which was balanced by the mortality rate. However, this balance was broken when the birth rate increased as the marriage rate increased. In addition, ongoing improvements in living standards and reductions in the death rate (particularly infant mortality) occurred in unison, so the population in the farming villages increased at a rate of over 1% a year. At first, there was room to expand the amount of arable acreage and introduce the techniques of intensive agriculture, and urban development drew large amounts of the population from the rural area. At the same time, farming villages were impacted by demand, which gave the increasing farming village population employment opportunities, so there was no need to hold the explosive population increase in check. On the other hand, the average household size in the villages, an indicator of the spread of small-scale operations, rapidly shrunk. In the latter half of the eighteenth century, it contracted to 4.0–4.5 people in almost every village. Also, it was not just that previously the average household size was large; the dispersed distribution came to be almost entirely concentrated in units of three to six people. This signified the establishment of the optimal management scale for agriculture and can be viewed as the result of economic behaviors on the part of the peasants.

5.4 Peasants and Production

How were these peasants connected to the economy? A bird's-eye view of the nationwide agricultural production during the Edo Period is a difficult matter. Using statistics from the early Meiji Period and local historical research, at the very least it can be said that in all areas specialty product zones suited to that locale were created. Naturally, the bulk of the *nengu* was paid in rice, so the peasants were unable to choose entirely economically feasible crops as a result of the difficulties of overland transport and the regulatory policies of the lord. However, it is dangerous to overrate the effects of the laws restricting crops imposed by the lord in the end. We must bear in mind that the general laws enacted by the shogunate during the Edo Period – not just these crop restriction laws – cannot be said to have been applied nationwide, and that the lords of the Edo Period lacked the administrative capacity to enforce these laws to the letter. The samurai class resided in the castle towns and toured the farming villages only when necessary, and the great majority of peasant life was carried out within an autonomous system in the village.

Roughly speaking, these specialty product zones can be described as follows. First, for cotton, the raw material used for making clothing, production zones were created primarily in the Kinai plain, as well as the Nōbi and Mikawa areas in the east, and the sandy soils of the Seto Inland Sea coastal areas in the west. Clearly, new farmland was developed for the purposes of cotton production. For the mulberries required in sericulture, production zones developed in the damp mountainous regions and gentle slopes of central Japan, with the primary areas in the southern part of Ōu, northern Kantō, Kai, Shinano, Echigo, and Mino Provinces. Division of labor progressed in the latter days of the Edo Period, with production zones for even silkworm-egg cards being created. Production zones for hemp were somewhat spread out throughout the northern Kantō area and the rest of Japan.

Along with cotton, rapeseed was a major commercial crop in the Kinai area. Rapeseed oil (liquid oil) was extremely effective, so large quantities of the oil were extracted. As far as sugar, white sugar was produced in areas such as northeastern Shikoku and southern Osaka, and brown sugar was a specialty product produced in the Satsuma Domain (more on this later). Indigo was important for dyeing, and Awa was well-known for it, but production areas formed in the Kantō region as well. The Tōhoku area had few specialty products, but safflowers were cultivated there, along with rush (*igusa*) in the plains areas, and wax trees (for making wax) in Western Japan and lacquer were cultivated on the slopes elsewhere.

Food, including rice, was also targeted for commercial production. Fresh vegetables became a specialty item in the areas around the cities. Rice was produced commercially in Hokuriku and Kyushu (which were single-crop zones), and rice from areas such as Kaga and Higo were traded at the Osaka market as "brand-name rice."

How the peasants interacted with markets in these types of specialty product zones is a thought-provoking issue. Conditions such as the type of produce and distance to the market varied greatly and cannot be easily characterized. However, it appears that the circumstances in the latter half of this period differed from that of the earlier half. During the period of market expansion in the first half, peasants were able to act on their own initiative even if through merchant intervention, but in the latter half, in many cases market expansion hit a ceiling. Seeking to monopolize supply in order to prevent consumer prices from dropping, the merchants organized *nakama* (guilds), and to monopolize demand toward the peasant–producers, they worked to keep purchase prices down. Disputes were created as a result, such as those between peasants and merchants regarding purchase price for rapeseed, a product that dominated the farming villages in the Kinai area during the latter half of the eighteenth century. These disputes occurred over a wide area (over 1,000 villages) and were akin to an appeal to the provincial authorities (known as *kokuso*).

5.5 The Rise of Landlordism

At any rate, it was inconceivable that the peasants were disenfranchised from economic opportunities, but it has been observed that even if they had successfully seized these opportunities and acquired wealth, they were not inclined toward becoming "wealthy farmers," as they did not reinvest this wealth to expand their businesses or boost production. If wealth were obtained without business expansion, they likely were forced in the direction of owning land to be cultivated by tenant cultivators (*kosaku*). In other words, "landowners" were born.

In a way, this can likely be explained as the dependence on family labor existing as the optimal technological system. Other forms of labor, servant labor, and employed labor were disadvantageous for their own unique reasons. Among these forms of labor, the disadvantages of servant labor have already been discussed. Now, let us take a look at employed labor.

Of course, it is not as though employed labor was not present in the agriculture of the Edo Period. Far from it, employees held an important role. However, on the other hand, it is a fact that the large-scale management that would have used this type of labor in large quantities did not exist at least as independent agriculture. This means that so-called economies of scale did not exist. Of course, operations that hired at the level of several employees can be found everywhere. There was also a change in the substance of employment: initially, an employment period was long, with low wages, and a substantial amount of goods and food were included in the pay. Also, many workers were employed seasonally over a period of many years. Later, employment was normally for a period of one year, with wages around four *ryō* a year (short-term seasonal employees). Also, there was much short-term labor, such as semi-annual seasonal employment, seasonal employment, and day labor, and throughout the Edo Period a tendency toward shortening employment periods can be seen. For the initial multi-year seasonal workers, we can assume that they retained their prior character as a servant labor force. Ultimately, increased employment opportunities accompanied economic development, and in particular, urban development was accompanied by the labor force being absorbed by the merchant and artisan sectors, which were relatively free of heavy physical labor, and this is likely the cause for old-style multi-year seasonal labor no longer being permitted. Consequently, a certain standard was created for employee wages, which in some cases resulted in great weight being placed on business expenses, which then became an obstacle to expansions in scale.

Also, under conditions where profit acquisition was close to its limit, in agriculture, where there were large seasonal differences in the demand for labor, retaining a large number of employees meant inefficiency for the operation. In cases where there was a level of labor sufficient to satisfy labor requirements during the farming season, it was likely to become a burden to operations during the off-season. When there was a level of labor sufficient to satisfy labor requirements during the off-season, it was extremely difficult to secure labor for the farming season in the labor market. The reason is that the farming season did not affect just the operation in question, it affected the entire region, and under conditions where transport methods were undeveloped, migrations to fulfill short-term labor demand from other regions were not possible to begin with. Operations dependent on servant labor likely did not suffer greatly from this kind of problem. The reason is that there were no elements of market competition for produce, and managers had little need to think about efficiency regarding labor premised on a low standard of living. Therefore, when a market economy developed and intensive agriculture was adopted, labor was likely based on family labor – a labor force that by nature was best able to respond to seasonal changes in the demand for labor. Methods such as partially supplementing family labor with employed labor and transplanted labor (known as *yui* (cooperative work group in rice planting)) among the peasants during the peak periods were the optimal forms for overcoming labor shortages.

In conclusion to this matter, it must be pointed out that as opposed to the disadvantages of expanding operations, lending land was advantageous. In many cases, land ownership changed hands through forfeitures and foreclosures, but in this case, it was rare for even tenant cultivating rights to be lost. Even if ownership was lost, in many cases the person who put up the land as collateral retained cultivation rights. Even if this was not the case, it was also economically advantageous for the landowner to utilize the flexibility of family labor, form a tenant cultivating relationship, and collect rent. In particular, during the mid-Edo Period, when population increases continued and population pressures on arable land intensified, landowners could now take the initiative in setting tenant cultivating rents, and land ownership became advantageous due to its scarcity value. Then, once these types of relationships were established, the relationship between landowners and tenant cultivators was not merely an economic one, but also came to function as a social relationship and even as a status relationship. Here is the prototype of the "landowner system" that characterized pre-World War II Japan.

In the end, the fact that a shift in operations toward farming for profit did not occur regardless of the expansion in economic opportunities can only be explained from the character of small-scale operations, where economically there are no economies of scale, but rather a type of "law of diminishing returns" at work. Also, it was precisely the dependence on family labor, a non-market supply-and-demand system, that was the basic model of labor supply for Edo Period agriculture.

5.6 Peasant Migration

However, despite the dependence on this type of a non-market supply-and-demand system in the agricultural realm, there were frequent regional labor migrations on the part of rural village residents. In terms of the system, it is often said that as serfs, the peasants were bound to their land and did not have freedom of movement. However, unlike medieval Western Europe, where there was this type of bondage to the land, the lord did not directly manage the land, and there were many opportunities for migration due to conditions such as the economic development in urban areas and the permeation of economic society. However, urban life was unhealthy and prone to the influences of contagious diseases and famine at the time, and viewed over the long-term, the death rate exceeded the birth rate, so a constant population influx from the farming villages was required. Cities during the Edo Period (which can be understood as densely populated areas) were also no exception. For example, in a survey conducted by the *bakufu* government during the latter days of the Edo Period, over one-fourth of Edo residents were born in farming villages. Not to mention that during the first half of this period, which was a period of rapid increase for the urban population, there must have been a great deal of migration from the farming villages into the cities.

Also, there were many temporary migrations. In local studies of farming villages in Shinano, the situation at the beginning of the nineteenth century (when there was the greatest number of work-related migrations) was that 30% of the working-age male population living in farming villages had moved to Edo to work. Also, in studies of the farming villages in the Nōbi region as well (Hayami 2010), among the peasants born there during the same period, two-thirds of those who survived to the age of 11 (approximately 75% of births) had relocated to find work, and among those who had relocated to find work, over two-thirds chose cities and towns as their destinations. And, among those who migrated to the cities to find work, approximately one-third of them either relocated or died there, not returning to the villages.

This type of mass labor migration from the farming villages to the cities – whether it was for a permanent relocation or just to work – is a key point that has been overlooked by studies thus far. Naturally, this does not mean that the peasants had complete freedom of movement. As a matter of form, these migrations required a certificate called a *ninbetsuokuri*. However, in many cases people migrated without even having this certificate, and in birthplace records these people were classified as being "unaccounted for."

Then, why did the peasants migrate to the cities? One probable reason is that there was increased employment in the cities, so working for at least several years prior to marriage and accumulating some savings, or giving their parents greater financial security, would have been difficult as long as they remained in the farming villages. Also, cities offered freedom of consumption. People were able to live their lives irrespective of their origins or family status. Truly, "city air created freedom." Therefore, cities had the social and economic attraction to lure people away from the farming villages. Put in somewhat exaggerated terms, cities were akin to a Venus flytrap which lured its prey and killed it. From the standpoint of the peasants, going to the cities was a choice of whether to bear the risk of death in exchange for a passing moment of freedom.

5.7 Peasant Life

Much has been written about life and conditions inside rural villages. What is important is that the "village" during the Edo Period was simultaneously an administrative unit as well as a living unit. Throughout Japanese history, the relationship between villages being both administrative and living units is a feature found only in the Edo Period. This speaks to the fact that the aspects of the "village" as a living community were unified with the aspects it possessed backed by official authority established through the *murauke nengu* system. Therefore, during this period the "village" was an extremely strong system. The lord recognized the autonomous authority of the "villages" – for example, the handling within the village of incidents that occurred in the village, was standard practice, which meant that village officials such as *shōya* or *nanushi* (village headman) had a great deal of authority. They were the leaders who maintained order in the village as a community, while being in a position where they were the interface for official authority, performing duties such as transmitting official orders, collecting *nengu*, and exercising judicial power. They had much greater authority than the executives of modern prefectural and municipal governments. Therefore, who would assume the position of village official was an important matter. Generally, village officials were chosen from within the village and approved by the lord. However, among them there were some who were like bureaucrats and were appointed, and even transferred, by the lord, as was the case in the Tosa Domain. Within the village, there were also cases where one family would serve as village officials for generations, but in many cases, the appropriate candidate was selected from among several families who could serve as village officials, taking age and opinions into consideration. Also, deputies known as *kimoiri* and *kumigashira* (head of the *goningumi*) were appointed with equal authority to the *shōya* and *nanushi*. In the areas directly controlled by the shogunate, the *hyakushōdai* (farmers' representative) represented the interests of ordinary peasants and acted as auditors, checking whether the village officials were committing any improprieties.

Ordinary peasants normally had a status known as *honbyakushō* (landowner farmers). Originally, at the beginning of the Edo Period (or right before it) this status was a name used for families obligated to provide the lord with compulsory labor. Although it was called "compulsory labor," the purpose was not peacetime agricultural labor; these levies primarily consisted of supplying temporary labor and civil works projects during wartime. When the Warring States Period reached its end, battles were generally carried out in places far removed from the lord's base, and transport, etc. required a large amount of physical labor besides the labor of those directly engaged in fighting, so compulsory peasant labor was applied. Also, the latter part of the Warring States Period and the early Edo Period was the time when a large number of public works projects such as castle, city, road and bridge, and flood control/irrigation construction projects were carried out. Compulsory peasant labor is assumed to be the source of the unskilled labor for these projects. There is a famous phrase that tells the story of the peasants at the beginning of the early modern period – *hyakushōdomo kutabire mōshisōrō* (The peasants are exhausted) – since Hideyoshi conscripted large numbers of them into service.

This means that initially compulsory labor was that important, and the ability to provide labor was frequently investigated. In most domains, this was assessed by subtracting from peasant households those who were not required to provide labor (such as village officials, persons affiliated with temples and shrines, artisans, etc.) and those who were incapable of providing labor (for example, *nago, ge'nin*, the physically disabled, widows, and the elderly, etc.), and those who remained were deemed *honbyakushō* . The method adopted assessed the obligation based on the number of *honbyakushō* – almost like determining the amount of *nengu* by multiplying the *nengu* rate by the *kokudaka*. Therefore, initially *honbyakushō* was a family lineage (or a social status) obliged to provide compulsory labor.

However, the obligation to provide the lord with compulsory labor faded in necessity with the arrival of the *pax Tokugawa*, so this obligation was converted to rice and monetary taxes. The nature of the *honbyakushō* changed as well. One matter was that the lord took an interest in the peasants' land holdings (through laws such as those eternally prohibiting the sale of land and those restricting subdividing land). Also, once the peasants primarily became the ones to bear the primary *nengu*, the term *honbyakushō* came to refer to peasants who owned land and had *nengu* obligations. In other words, *honbyakushō* equaled *takamochibyakushō* (landholding peasants). Even within the village, two systems were created: an order based on lineage and family status, and a system based on the size of their land, i.e., their land holdings. In addition to the expected *nengu* paid to the lord and any supplemental taxes, village accounts (*murairiyō*) also came to be assessed based on land holdings (from being assessed based on household status to being assessed by land holdings). As such, the presence or amount of landholdings became extremely significant in ranking peasants.

Thus, *honbyakushō* signified land-holding peasants without regard to the size of these holdings. Major landowners with several hectares of land and *de facto* tenant cultivators who owned a mere fraction of that both held *honbyakushō* status. As far as the lords were concerned, the *honbyakushō* were the ones ultimately obligated to pay *nengu*, so the category of *honbyakushō* was frequently used in various surveys and procedures. Since this is how it has been recorded in numerous documents, modern scholars also like to use the term *honbyakushō*, but we must bear in mind that it clearly does not refer to a class where economic and social interests were held in common.

In contrast, peasants called *mudaka* and *mizunomi* did not own land, and simultaneously formed a social and economic class. In other words, they were tenant cultivators. However, even among the *honbyakushō*, those with only meager amounts of land in reality had to act as tenant cultivators. Despite the frequent references to the segmentation of the peasant class, the number of *mudaka* and *mizunomi* in Edo Period records is surprisingly low. If we assume that there was extreme segmentation, as has been said, the number or proportion of *mudaka* and *mizunomi* would have to be much higher. Even if we assume as fact that powers that created differentiation were at work, then some kind of reverse power that blocked segmentation may have been at work. Following the process where peasants who were formerly *honbyakushō* lost their land, in almost all cases they ultimately retained their homes. Residential land was also treated the same way as farmland for *nengu* purposes, so even peasants who kept only their homes were ranked as *honbyakushō*. These kinds of circumstances were also in play, but the presence of the family system in Japan is of greater importance. The peasant households that appear in historical documents are treated as though each one acts as an independent operating body, but in reality, this was not the case. Several households gathered to create a family body related by blood and acted under its constraints. For example, it is safe to say that the relationship between the main-line family (*honke*) and branch families (*bunke*) very strongly regulated the social life of the peasants. While the branch families were subordinate to the main line in several aspects, the main line was customarily obligated to protect the branch families. When a branch family lost its land for one reason or another and was on the verge of collapse, it was often likely that the main line would provide them with support. These types of social relationships are omitted when the segmentation of the peasant class during this period is observed from only an economic standpoint. The infiltration of economic society into the farming villages must not be perceived as mechanical. The family system, far from being destroyed by economic society, can instead be viewed as having been bolstered by it, something that requires explanation.

This peasant class was by no means a single class, but along with the dismantlement of large-scale operations, the peasants stood for common interests as an operational body, and with the exception of a mere handful of major landowners, they were all working peasants. As they formed a community built upon these interests, exclusion from this community practically threatened one's survival. The degree of suffering from the punishment of ostracism (*mura hachibu*) was nothing at all like what it is today. From matters directly related to daily production, such as usufructuary rights pertaining to irrigation water and wastewater, use of common lands, and road maintenance, to festivals and ceremonies – peasant families during the Edo Period were so firmly embedded into their communities that leaving them and acting independently was inconceivable. However, in the end it is dangerous to excessively appraise the regulations imposed by the family system and these community organizations. Even assuming there were various differences in the level of whatever room was left, peasants were able to behave as independent agents. Although it cannot be said that all peasants were able to avail themselves of this, it is something that can be considered economic individualism. However little, attention is being paid to growth in this area instead.

As a result, during the latter half of this period, hard-working peasants known as *tokunō* (exemplary farmers) appeared nationwide. They devised a most rational production system based on experience, and in some cases they recorded this system in an attempt to objectify it. This meant the creation of agricultural texts, and agricultural science. Even if this was not the case, numerous printed texts and almanacs related to farming created during the Edo Period will be discovered through modern documentary research on farming villages. Although modern scientific viewpoints will take issue with its content, the peasants were actively engaged in production; it is not the case that the peasants were under the control of their relatives and village laws and had no autonomy, and continuously produced in accordance with custom. Among them, quite a few kept business records and farming diaries, but this can also be considered a product of their efforts and attitudes toward rationalizing production.

5.8 Demography in the Latter Half of the Edo Period

It is often said that there was economic stagnation during the latter half of the Edo Period. Without a doubt, the rapid economic expansion of the first half was long gone. More than anything, the urban population ceased to increase, and expansion in consumer demand slowed down. Developments in intensive agricultural technology also reached its limits for its time, and population increases conversely became a source of pressure, which threatened people's livelihoods in some areas. However, it is a mistake to uniformly apply this "stagnation" aspect nationwide. It is difficult to examine economic development or stagnation regionally, but fortunately we are able to use the province-by-province numbers in the nationwide censuses performed by the Tokugawa bakufu (Sekiyama 1957). Now we will utilize these numbers and attempt to perform an economic analysis of the latter half of the Edo Period on a regional basis.

As part of the Kyōhō Reforms, in 1721 the shogunate ordered the *daimyō*, *hatamoto*, and *daikan* to request population data on the commoners under their control, and from 1726 onward, a similar report was ordered once every six years (during the years of the rat and the horse). Today, as far as we can tell, the final count was in 1846, and there are signs that reports were requested in 1852 as well. We are able to use the provincial data for the 12 censuses performed during this period. However, how reliable are the results of these censuses? Although this is the case with any statistical data, particularly in historical statistics prior to the establishment of modern statistical systems, the numerical data must be carefully examined, and forgoing this step is equal to losing the basis for an argument. First, we must remember that these numbers are not of the entire population and included various excluded and redundant segments of the population. Redundancy has already been discussed. As far as the exclusions, this does not include the samurai population as an excluded class. Furthermore, these surveys did not have a common methodology, and the results based on survey methods previously performed by the lord were tabulated without correction.

This resulted in infants and juveniles being excluded in some domains. In Kanazawa Domain, people age 15 or younger were excluded, and in Wakayama Domain, only those eight or older were counted. Therefore, these numbers are markedly inaccurate as an absolute value. Therefore, the desirable method in using this data is to assume that same method was used in the same region, and make a relative comparison by region and era. The results obtained through this method satisfy our present objectives. Fortunately, we can obtain the numbers by province for the years close to the boundaries of these surveys, and Fig. 5.1 shows the rate of change between both years. Viewing this diagram, the first thing we can say is that in the population changes there was regional variation to a considerable extent in each region. Of course, there were also several exceptions, but generally a region showed the same tendencies.

Roughly speaking, the population in the Ōu and Kantō regions (henceforth, "East Japan") decreased; the Chūgoku, Shikoku, and Kyushu regions (henceforth, "West Japan," with the remainder as "Central Japan") increased and the central areas, Hokuriku, showed an increase; and the Tōkai and Kinki regions either stagnated or increased slightly. The areas that showed the most intense fluctuations were the Kōzuke, Shimotsuke, and Hitachi Provinces in northern Kantō, and Bizen, Bitchū, Bingo, Aki, Suō, and Nagato Provinces in the San'yō region (except Mimasaka). Expressed in real numbers, between both years the population in northern Kantō decreased from 1.84 million to 1.33 million, and in contrast, there was an increase of almost equal scale in San'yō, from 1.83 million to 2.27 million. Although there was virtually no change in the sum for both regions, the distribution greatly changed.

This example is an extreme case, but it is clear that conditions of population "stagnation" should not be considered to be uniform nationwide. In the case in San'yō, where population increases continued even in the latter half of the Edo Period (1.7‰ increase annually) and the case in northern Kantō, which showed a decrease (2.0‰ decrease annually), it is certain that the economic relationships were likely different.

Why did these regional differences in population trends occur? Population fluctuations are projected onto people's lives in diverse environmental changes, and they are not always solely the result of economic conditions. However, ascertaining what causes those fluctuations is necessary when considering the relationship between economy and population. As can be seen in Fig. 5.1, northeastern Japan – in particular, on the Pacific Ocean side – had marked decreases, and even within the same Ōu region, only a slight increase can be observed on the Sea of Japan side. This type of decrease resembles crop damage conditions due to damage from cold. If this is the case, this decrease appears to have a relationship to temperature decreases in the summer. Then, if we recall that the massive crop failure that afflicted Japan in the 1780s wreaked havoc on northeastern Japan, we can find the cause in the lower crop yields brought about by long-term drops in temperature. The Ōu region was the northernmost limit for the rice cultivation technology of the time, and it was a region particularly susceptible to the slightest change in temperature. In contrast, the Sea of Japan side of the same region was not as severely affected as the

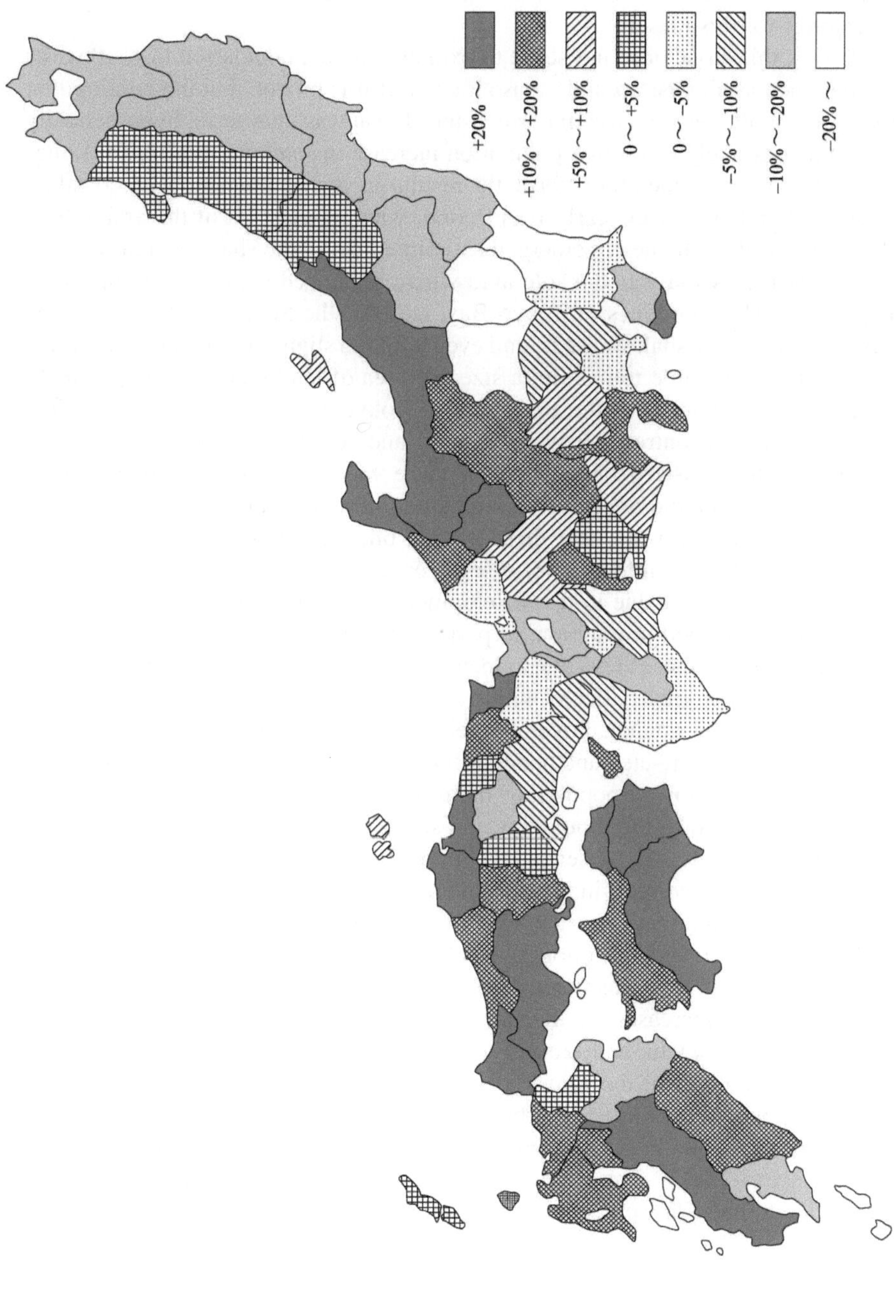

Fig. 5.1 Percentage of population change by province, 1721–1846

Pacific Ocean side, since the air currents from the high-pressure centers in the Sea of Okhotsk that caused cold-weather damage were blocked by the mountains. Also, central and southwestern Japan were largely spared the effects of lower summer temperatures for this reason.

However, this alone does not serve to explain why the population in southwestern Japan increased. One possible reason is that if it is proven that the cooling that caused the population decrease in northeastern Japan was long-term, hypothetically this would conversely result in a population increase in southwestern Japan. Long-term decreases in temperature normally results in the phenomenon of coastline regression. For Japan of the early Edo Period, where almost all of the arable land had been cultivated, the newly emerged shoreline land in the shallow areas created by shoreline regression was the sole area where organized expansion of farmland was possible. The shorelines of Tokyo Bay, Ise Bay, the Seto Inland Sea, and the Ariake Sea had many shallow areas, and even with the slightest amount of shoreline recession it was possible to reclaim a sizeable area of land without any new technologies in particular. With the exception of Tokyo Bay, most of these shallow shorelines were concentrated between central and southwestern Japan, and there were none in northeastern Japan. Even if there was some shoreline recession in northeastern Japan, it did not result in increased farmland via reclamation.

However, it is also a fact that these natural phenomena alone cannot serve as explanatory factors. Therefore, as a societal reason, we must consider the increase in employment capacity due to the development of manufacturing industries other than agriculture or food production, in particular, handicrafts. Southwestern Japan had the advantage in these areas due to materials and climate. Looking at population fluctuations in even greater detail within a province or region, even in provinces where the population stagnated overall, there were increases in regions where commercial crops were cultivated and handicraft industries were developed. Conversely, even in areas that showed population increases (as a province), cases where the population decreased in the mountains and single-crop wet-paddy rice field zones can be detected. Thus, the presence of commercial crop cultivation, and the presence of developed handicraft industries naturally affected population distribution.

Furthermore – and this is something that has already been discussed – attention must be paid to the fact that economic development invited urban development, and when its population ratio was pushed up, the death rate also rose, which served to check population increases in the area overall. The Kinai region (Yamashiro, Yamato, Settsu, Kawachi, and Izumi Provinces) had the greatest urban population ratios in the latter half of the Edo Period (in statistics from the early Meiji years, 33% of the population resided in urban areas with populations of 5,000 or more), followed by the southern Kantō region (Musashi, Sagami, Kazusa, Shimōsa, and Awa Provinces – 20%).[1] The chart shows that these regions, along with their surrounding areas, had a low percentage of population increase. The low percentage of

[1] According to the *Kyōbu seihyō*, an early Meiji Period population and commodities survey.

population increase in both of these regions, where economic development was most pronounced, can likely be understood this way. There were the restrictions described earlier, and since long-distance population migrations were difficult, the scope of population absorption in the major cities was in Kantō and its surroundings (Edo) and in the Kinai area and its surroundings (Kyoto and Osaka). It is likely these reasons that created the population trends in these regions, and the disparities with Hokuriku and southwestern Japan, which were less affected.

Thus, population trends are the result of several reasons, and drastic population decreases were seen in areas affected by both natural and social factors, such as in northern Kantō.

This time, these population fluctuations lent a different impact to the local economies. In regions that saw decreases due to natural causes, such as northeastern Japan, this was at the same time also a tragic experience for the peasants (for studies on population control, see Takahashi 1941–62). Population control measures such as abortions and infanticide were certainly not carried out willingly but were inevitable behaviors in order to survive. These can likely be understood as the result of threats to maintaining living standards. As a result, product purchasing power in that region conspicuously fell and economic activity unmistakably entered a severe, long-term stagnation. With the exception of a few specialty-product zones, such as sericulture and silk reeling, these regions were beset by circumstances that can be characterized as impoverished and tragic.

Nonetheless, we cannot simply state that areas with population increases saw economic development. There is no shortage of cases where population increases conversely placed pressure on the economic environment. However, when compared to northeastern Japan, which saw population decreases for the reasons stated earlier, the potential for market expansion and market activity stimulation remained in regions with population increases. During the latter half of the Edo Period, a great deal of the land holdings of the *bakufu* was concentrated in northeastern Japan, which worsened the financial situation. This was accompanied by sluggish growth in the Edo consumer market, which can also be assumed to have reduced economic activity in Osaka. Also, recent studies observe that there was relative regional and domain-level economic development, primarily in the cities in the domains in southwestern Japan. Naturally, this type of development in commercial goods production did not always mean profits for the peasants and ordinary merchants. As will be discussed later, there were cases where a domain monopolized distribution and sales, severing contact between the producer–peasants and the market, such as with the Satsuma sugar monopoly. Here, the economic and social standing of the peasants dropped significantly. However, cases where domain monopolies of this type succeeded were the exception rather than the norm, and it was difficult in regions adjoining central marketplaces. Therefore, for the most part, between the central areas and southwestern Japan, economic development and population increases were able to continue during the latter half of the Edo Period as well, and there is no need to link apparent stagnations in the nationwide population to economic stagnation.

5.9 Decline of the Lord's Economy

As demonstrated earlier, the circulation of currency and assets crossed over into all strata of Edo Period society, and even the samurai class was not an exception. However, compared with the other social classes, the middle and lower samurai were ultimately unable to seize economic opportunities, and during the Edo Period, not one accumulated wealth and generated a fortune. Circumstances where those with political power are unable to seize economic opportunities are curious indeed. The reason is that, introducing political power into economic activity and attaining wealth is frequently seen in other countries. This fact demonstrates that in Edo Period Japan, political value was separate from economic value, and it should be seen as having a major influence on Japan's modernization. Now we shall look at the particulars of the economic situation of the samurai class during the Edo Period, and the course of its decline.

Looking at lords' finances during the Edo Period, they were perennially beset by deficits. Whether it was the shogunate or the *daimyō* or the *hatamoto*, during the Edo Period all lords' finances were strained, and the period ultimately came to an end without the fundamental problems being resolved. Rather, one is almost amazed that the *bakuhan* system was maintained for so long under such unsound finances.

These lords' financial deficits during the Edo Period were basically carried over from those under the wartime system during the Warring States Period. More than anything else, preparing for wars and having a large number of retainers to carry them out, and seizing an opponent's assets and land through winning battles was folded into the lords' finances of the Warring States Period. One explanation for Hideyoshi's reckless Korean campaign is that since he unified the nation and no longer had anything to seize, he had no other way to balance the nation's finances. Under the Tokugawa shogunate maintaining order was paramount, and since the conditions of the so-called *sakoku* (national isolation) were imposed, this problem became an internal matter for lords' finances. At first, the shogunate had some assets (in particular, an accumulation of precious metals) so they were not in any particular financial trouble, and they were even able to aid the *daimyō* and *hatamoto* who fell upon hard times, but these resources gradually dried up.

The primary reason for these financial difficulties is that there were too many vassals. Including their families, their numbers likely accounted for 7–8% of the total population. However, in an era of peace that lasted for more than two centuries, employing many vassals – who were originally professional soldiers – was a meaningless expense. Naturally, the *bakuhan* system was a political system, and samurai were needed to serve as administrators, but they were far too many in number. The samurai known as *bankata* (who staffed the shogunate's standing army) who were unable to secure positions as *yakukata* (those who filled the civil service) had to spend their days in idleness. In the case of the shogunate, *kobushin'iri* (taking a post created as an employment relief measure for low-ranking samurai) did not mean that they actually assumed the post, it meant that they did not have to do any substantial work. It might be said that during the Edo Period, procedures were made complicated and ceremonies became more rigid in order to provide work to this large number of unemployed samurai. At any rate, the masters could not fire their vassals just because they were having financial difficulties. The relationship between master and vassal was at the same time a relationship between a protector and the protected, and this principle persisted to the very end. A prominent example would be the Uesugi, a *daimyō* clan. The Uesugi had over one million *koku*, but their holdings were reduced to 300,000 *koku* in Yonezawa. However, they continued to maintain their original group of vassals.

Under financial conditions where lords employ such large numbers of vassals and become impoverished, Confucian morals were useful in maintaining master–vassal relations. A worldview where poverty was glorified and the acquisition of wealth scorned became the soul of the samurai, and they had to endure it for the sake of their master's households.

The second reason is an increase in expenditures. As a result of the warriors and farmers being separated, the samurai resided in the cities, and furthermore, as peace persisted, they gradually demanded splendor in their lives, so expenditures for culture and education increased. They were unable to raise their incomes (stipends) from their links to the *kokudaka* system, so they had to cut household expenses and make do with their fixed incomes, meaning they had virtually no way to make up for these increased expenditures. Even if it were possible to increase their *nengu* amount to a certain degree, after land tax rates were fixed, at the very least the amount of *nengu* they received from the peasants was practically fixed.

Third is the worsening imbalance between income and expenditure. Samurai incomes were in the form of currency and rice, but the rice was sold to brokers who dealt with the samurai (known as *fudasashi* and financier(*kakeya*)), and with the added currency they obtained they bought daily essentials. Therefore, fluctuations in the price of rice, and fluctuations in all other ordinary prices, worked to the samurais' disadvantage. Yet, from the mid-Edo Period onward, the price of rice was fixed for a long time, in contrast to prices in general, which inched upward. Phrased differently, the relative price gap between these two meant an increase in the samurais' financial burden.

As seen above, in a manner of speaking these financial difficulties can be seen as the logical outcome. As a result, the samurai class as a whole was impoverished, but the mid- to low-ranking samurai were hit the hardest. During the latter days of Edo Period, a majority of them, like the *hatamoto* residing in Edo declared *goshihōgae* – which today would be considered a type of bankruptcy – and they lived meager lives under the watchful eye of the merchants' accountants, retaining only an empty sense of status. Having no other source of income, this class of samurai ultimately lost the weapons, horses, and personnel they had to maintain as samurai, and ended up having to subcontract out family members to work as artisans.

The economic ruin of the *hatamoto* class was as follows. First, unable to resolve their increased expenditures, they received loans from the *fudasashi* and financier, putting up the following year's *nengu* income as collateral. However, as they had no means to increase their income, once they borrowed money, their debts inevitably snowballed. In order to help them out of this predicament, their master the shogunate provided aid, or ordered the cancellation of debts (or reductions in interest rates). However, this was a temporary solution and did not resolve the underlying problem. Also, in the end samurai finances had to rely on the *fudasashi* and financier, and debt-cancellation orders were a shock to them, conversely making samurai finance even more difficult.

Thus, with no further recourse, the *hatamoto* ultimately received bankruptcy protection. In this system the *hatamoto* were forced to live within their means: their assets were placed under the management of the merchants they were indebted to, and from that point forth the *hatamoto* lost the right to collect *nengu* from their fiefdoms, and the merchants formed a type of management organization with the village officials in the fiefdom. The merchants received the *nengu* directly, from which they paid a fixed allowance to the *hatamoto*. This was the mortgaging of lordship, and when this happened, it became unclear who was actually the lord.

5.10 Solutions to the Financial Crisis

The shogunate and *daimyō* could not stand idly by during this financial crisis. As might be expected, various solutions were attempted, but their effectiveness is another matter. These solutions are presented below, starting with the "negative" ones.

First, once the authorities became aware of the financial crisis, of course sumptuary laws were issued and reinforced. Since the Confucian teachings they adopted as their ideology naturally viewed frugality as a virtue, these orders were easily issued. Frugality was called for in all aspects of life, but since these laws naturally applied to those outside of the samurai class as well, they had a certain economic impact, in particular, on the consumption of goods that were regarded as luxury items at the time, such as high-quality silk goods. However, these were not problems of a level that were solved through this type of psychological regulation.

Next were spending cuts, particularly cuts to the stipends and allowances that occupied a major portion of expenditures. These were reduced by a fixed percentage (for example, by half). The ability to implement these types of measures was due to the master–vassal relationship that held them together and would be unthinkable today.

The aforementioned measures were negative ones intended to maintain financial equilibrium entirely through spending cuts. However, increased *nengu* collections were constantly attempted as a "positive" measure to attain equilibrium by increasing revenue. Other such measures are described below.

First, the devaluation of currency and the issuance of domain currencies were already described in the section on the currency system. These measures temporarily had a significant effect: for example, the profits (which at the time were labeled as *deme*, or the proceeds from recoinage) from the devaluation during the Genroku Period (for example, the gold content of a one-*ryō koban* was reduced from 84.3 to 57.4%, approximately two-thirds) reached five million *ryō*. Since the shogunate's ordinary revenue at the time was approximately one million *ryō* a year, this truly means that they were able to attain the equivalent of five years' worth of income. The domains, which did not have minting rights, supplemented their income through issuing their own paper currency. However, these measures were merely temporary; the currency devaluations during the first half of the Edo Period weakened its purchasing power, leading to a vicious spiral that caused price inflation.

Next were measures to seek income other than *nengu* – in other words, the *nengu* borne by the peasants – and the merchants were the ones most frequently targeted. Under the principles of free markets, open guilds, and free commerce, the merchants were not recognized as taxpayers, unlike the peasants. However, when economic revitalization made the merchants wealthy, the shogunate acted in an attempt to collect *nengu* from them through a variety of means. The merchants had to make compulsory donations known as *goyōkin* and required to provide low-interest loans for which they had no hope of being repaid. Also, the shogunate took advantage of circumstances where market expansion was stalled and authorized guilds granted them special privileges and collected merchant license fees (*myōga*) and commercial taxes (*unjō*) from them. This shows that in exchange for these payments the position of the merchants substantially improved, but for the seigneur, it was an inevitable concession as they were no longer able to collect *nengu* from the peasants above a fixed amount.

Taking an additional step forward, the lord class itself started to act as economic agents, particularly in the area of distribution. Domain monopolies were an example of this, and it was done by buying up the specialty products in their territory and then transporting them to the central markets for a profit. For this to succeed, several conditions had to exist simultaneously, and the Satsuma Domain's brown sugar monopoly during the latter days of the Edo Period – which will be discussed below – is also linked to the Meiji Restoration, with important implications (see Haraguchi 1966).

The Satsuma Domain's relationship with the *bakufu* was also precarious, and they were burdened with numerous government construction obligations and mired in debt. In the 1830s, their debts to the Osaka merchants reached an astonishing sum. Zusho Hirosato, who was responsible for reforms, noticed that the brown sugar being produced in the Satsuma's territories was not produced elsewhere, so he made it so that the domain had a monopoly over it. Sugar producers were unable to sell sugar to anyone other than the domain (designated sugar brokers), so the domain monopolized the purchase of sugar, buying it at a low price and issuing vouchers as payment. This sugar was transported to Osaka on ships with sails bearing the domain's official seal. In Osaka, the domain, this time as the sole supplier, was able to sell the sugar at a high price. The domain used a portion of the proceeds to purchase essentials for the peasants, which they then transported back to their domain, and sold to the peasants in exchange for the vouchers. This allowed the domain to secure enormous profits and repay their debts within a short period of time, saving them from bankruptcy. Ultimately, they succeeded by restricting the movements of the peasants and ordinary merchants in the production and distribution of brown sugar and cutting off their access to markets, and it can be said that it was the unique circumstances in the Satsuma Domain that made this method possible. The lord's monopolizing markets in this manner was impossible in Kantō and Kinai, where the markets were not geographically close, and a single lord did not control the territory outright, unlike the Satsuma Domain.

As shown above, successful monopolies could be seen only in a limited number of domains, but the fact that the influential domains in the southwest rescued the finances of their domains to varying degrees through this method cannot be dismissed as an exception when its relationship to the Meiji Restoration is considered.

5.11 Shogunate Governmental Reforms

In order to examine specifically how reforms were carried out in the shogunate and domain governments, we will look at the economic aspects of the Kyōho Reforms (a typical example) by the shogunate, and those by the father and son team of Tanuma Okitsugu and Okitomo decades later (known as the "Tanuma Era").

The Kyōho Reforms were a series of shogunate governmental reforms carried out under the direct supervision of the shogun Yoshimune. The reforms with deep economic connections can be grouped as follows: (1) *nengu* system reforms, (2) land, peasant, and agricultural policies, (3) merchant and commerce policies, and (4) currency and price policies.

First, the reforms to the *nengu* system: a shift was made from the previous method known as *kemidori*, where the *nengu* assessment was determined by surveying the quality of the harvest every year, to one known as *jōmendori*, where the *nengu* rate for a defined period was fixed (provided there was not a particularly bad harvest). Prior historians have characterized this as a policy to increase *nengu* collections (see for example Ōishi 1961). The *kemi* (field inspection) system surveyed the quality of the crop each year, determined the rate, multiplied it by the *muradaka*, and determined the *nengu* amount of the village, so it was an assessment method capable of responding to short-term fluctuations in yield. In contrast, the fixed-rate method determined the fixed rate for a defined period of 10 or 20 years (in reality, for extended periods of several decades or more), so the official *nengu* amount borne by the peasants became fixed, as long as there was no change to their *kokudaka* or *muradaka*. Definitely in the short term – and the long-term as well – there would have been no problem with fixing the *nengu* amount in this manner under conditions where there were no increases in production. However, should there have been long-term increases in yield, this system would have relatively lowered the percentage occupied by the *nengu* in the whole production yield. One may wonder if there were no increases in yield during the latter half of the Edo Period, but increases were seen in a majority of regions, except northeastern Japan. In this regard, whatever the shogunate's designs may have been, they were likely unable to link the significance of implementing the fixed-rate system to increased *nengu* collections. However, we must remember that this type of shift in the *nengu* collection method took place at a time when the initial trend toward production increases finally tapered off. Also, at this point the urban population was at its limit, and the increase in the food-consuming population reached the maximum. Therefore, at the very least rice consumption reached its limit, and rice prices at the Osaka market remained level for an extended period. Thus, supplying large quantities of *nengu* rice to the market posed the risk of causing prices to collapse. These circumstances must be considered as background to the implementation of the fixed-rate system.

Also, the previous field inspection system had to perform surveys of the rice crops in each village annually, but precise surveys were difficult; moreover, they were performed only on rice, so no assessments whatsoever were performed on commercial crops other than rice, which were gradually increasing. It might be said that for the shogunate, disposing of this complex and ineffective method may have been easy under the conditions described above.

If we assume that implementing the fixed-rate system in this way did not lead to increased *nengu* collections, as is often said, what kind of meaning can we ascribe to it? We might be able to take it as a policy intended to stabilize *nengu* income. The field inspection method could only ascertain *nengu* income in its entirety for a certain point in time, but with the fixed-rate method, at least rice quantities could be established. Since rice prices also tended to be fixed over a long period of time, the shogunate was able to estimate the amount of *nengu* income this way. In that sense, the fixed-rate method was a policy to stabilize *nengu* income, or to introduce a budgetary system, but not to increase it. As might be expected, the shogunate was gasping under the weight of its financial difficulties and had to seek out income sources other than the *nengu* from the peasants.

On the other hand, since the implementation of the fixed-rate system meant that *nengu* obligations were fixed for the peasants as well, this could be viewed as favorable conditions being bestowed upon the peasants in general. A fixed parcel of land having fixed *nengu* obligations (the actual standards aside) made calculating profits in agricultural operations convenient in a sense.

The encouragement of new field development and the revision of laws pertaining to pledged land can be listed as examples in the second category: the land, peasant, and agricultural policies. By implementing the fixed-rate system, increased *nengu* income from existing farmland could no longer be expected, so increases in farmland were encouraged and were used as a source of income. New field development had always been encouraged, but during the Kyōho Reforms they differed from previous cases. Before the Kyōho Reforms, from the relationship with small farmer independence policies, ownership of the newly developed land by the landowner class was not desirable. Also, new field development proceeded under the condition that it would not be a hindrance to production in the primary fields. For these two reasons, it is not as though development were unrestricted, at least in principle. In these reforms, new field development was encouraged taking the creation of the new landowner class into account. In other words, development by the townsmen was permitted. In this regard, the Kyōhō Reforms signified a shift in how the peasants were viewed, although the actual substance is a different matter.

Besides these, there were revisions to the laws regarding the handling of pledged land, but it is well known that these caused confusion and ended in failure.

Third, regarding merchants and commerce, as part of the price control measures to be described below, merchants were permitted to form organizations, and policies from the beginning of the shogunate prohibiting free trade and the formation of guilds was changed. This was the first move toward official recognition of a type of monopoly organization, which would later directly lead to the formation of protective organizations known as *kabunakama*. At the same time merchants started to be regulated, this also established the position of the merchants. The shogunate's immediate objective in authorizing these merchant organizations was to use them to keep prices in check. Associations were organized for individual products, and it was expected that they would set maximum prices, and keep them under control. The result cannot be said to have been successful, of course, but the fact that merchants' associations were organized after a period of market expansion had in the end resulted in the formation of monopoly organizations by these associations supplying commodities.

As already stated, the fourth monetary policy was to improve the standing of currency, and reduce the amount of issued currency circulation, similar to the recoinage during the Shōtoku years. This is what was most faithful to the spirit of the Kyōhō Reforms. However, these types of currency reforms were not accepted since they had the adverse effect of contracting economic activity, so they were ultimately withdrawn. The era of coordinated debasements had begun.

Now, the following can be said when the Kyōho Reforms are taken as whole. At a time when almost no scientific inquiries were made on economic phenomena, it should come as no surprise that economic policies were riddled with contradictions. It is often said that the spirit of these reforms were conservative in nature, and the ultimate objective was to rein in the extravagant lifestyles of the samurai in peacetime, and maintain financial equilibrium by returning to the days of Ieyasu. By nature, it was a type of contracted equilibrium, and it assumed that a contraction in economic activity was unavoidable. Nevertheless, on the one hand, the development of new fields which led to expansion and some commercial crop cultivation were encouraged. Also, it had already become impossible to prohibit or restrict economic activity by the merchants. Therefore, the intent of the Kyōho Reforms was definitely contracted equilibrium, and in particular, frugality was demanded of the samurai class. However, in reality contractions in economic activity were no longer tolerated, and ultimately the gap between the intent and reality of the reforms made them unpopular.

The Tanuma years are often observed as being open in character and having finances with expanding equilibrium, as opposed to the conservative character and contracting equilibrium of the Kyōho Reforms. Moral assessments of Tanuma Okitsugu aside, he must be acknowledged as a proponent of economic development – something rarely seen in the framework of Tokugawa *bakuhan* society – and as a politician who implemented it.

The official recognition of the protective organizations is likely his best-known policy. Already in the Kyōho Reforms, the protective organizations were recognized with the intention to control prices, but he took it one step further to create monopoly organizations at every level of transaction for every product, from which commercial taxes and merchant license fees were collected. With this, the monopoly organizations were accompanied by force backed by official authority, and outsiders were forced into disadvantageous circumstances. Tanuma was famous for taking bribes due to these official recognitions. At a time when the tempo of market expansion had already dulled, the establishment of these types of monopoly organizations coincided with the interests of the merchants, so many people assume that Edo Period commerce automatically means protective organizations or monopoly control. Due to this, commercial acts clearly became a target for taxation, and the traditional views that disparaged commercial acts for not creating value greatly changed.

Tanuma also utilized the merchants' financial power and planned large-scale new field development. In the end, these plans did not come to fruition, but he formulated plans to reclaim the Teganuma and Inbanuma marshes using the wealth of the Edo and Osaka merchants. This was also a major shift from previous conservative thinking insofar as it attempted to use the wealth of merchants who could not find investment opportunities due to market contraction.

However, the largest reforms were those pertaining to the currency system and the trade and industry promotion policies linked to them. As previously illustrated, the currency system at one time minted engraved silver coins that indicated their value in gold. These coins were called *nanryōgin*. This currency was extremely convenient, unlike prior weighted currencies, and deeply permeated the lives of the commoners, but at the same time, this also meant that currency was no longer appraised by its precious metal value.

Copper was the primary export during this period, and the Dutch East Indies Company supplied a portion of it to the European markets, and copper was even used strategically. However, as a supplement, attention was paid to marine products – in particular, the *tawaramono sanpin* (three luxury marine products): dried abalone, shark's fin, and dried sea slug, which appeared after Arai Hakuseki implemented the Shōtoku reforms. Tanuma attempted to expand these, establishing *tawaramono kaisho* (luxury marine product centers) in areas nationwide, where product collection and capital loan services were provided. This was a type of export industry promotion policy, and these policies could be considered unprecedented for their time in that these measures were taken for industries other than agriculture (particularly rice). Yet, these types of products were primarily acquired through capture, and there were major technological restrictions, so the claim cannot be made that it had the effect of raising production levels over the long term.

The Tanuma years were a time when the breadth of economic policy was expanded to the extent that Tokugawa *bakuhan* society would tolerate. Therefore, the Tanumas were seen as heretics by the shogunate's conservative faction, and compounded by their bribe-taking, in the end both father and son were condemned. The reforms that followed were the conservative Kansei Reforms by Matsudaira Sadanobu. In addition, the swing of the pendulum from expansion to contraction dragged Japan into the Tempo Reforms (a time of contraction) from the Bunka and Bunsei eras (three decades of expansion in the early nineteenth century). Also, all of these eras plowed into the walls of the *bakuhan* system and faced setbacks, repeatedly moved in the opposite direction. We might say that the Meiji Restoration was a reform where this pendulum broke through the walls of the *bakuhan* system under conditions where the nation was opened up.

Then, what was the wall or framework of the *bakuhan* system? In principle, under the *bakuhan* system, the peasants were required to be economically self-sufficient, and production for sale was prohibited, but in reality, due to the separation of the farmers and warriors, the construction of castle towns, the alternate attendance system, and payment of *nengu* in rice as well as currency, as a condition they were allowed to produce for sale. Therefore, disparities in policies formed depending on whether government officials chose to respect principle or face reality. However, no matter how much one insisted on principle, the currency-based economy could not be dismissed; and even if one chose to respect reality, the *bakuhan* system itself could not be dismissed.

5.12 Social Anxiety

In an era such as the Edo Period, where economic opportunities were accorded to all strata of society, and each of these strata was influenced differently, it is only natural that social movements will form due to economic reasons. However, unlike today, in areas such as the transmission of information, means of transport, and the spread of education, people lived in very small worlds. Social movements were also individualistic and diffuse, and could not reach the level of a large movement capable of shaking the *bakuhan* system. However, for example, if we look carefully at the character of the local peasant uprisings (*ikki*), we see that the frequent revolts against the loss of clan rights previously held by the powerful peasants gradually shifted to the ordinary peasants, and at least at the local level, they began to display unity as a class. Questions began to arise regarding the fact that the relationship the peasants had with all other aspects had become an *economic* one, but the relationship with the lord was a subordinate one regarding *status*. However, in the end, the Meiji Restoration began without any movement clearly taking up this issue as rallying cry. Analysis of these movements requires the difficult task of probing into the many complex socioeconomic relationships in the background of a rallying cry (a modern classic on peasant uprisings is Kokushō 1928, but for a more comprehensive work, see White 1995).

Chapter 6
The Rise of Industriousness in Early Modern Japan

6.1 Introduction

The Japanese people are often said to be industrious (although this has recently become questionable). In particular, there are those who say this is due to the "national character" (*kokuminsei*) of the Japanese people. The author does not feel that the concept of "national character" is appropriate in all circumstances. The French term "mentalité" indicates the basic psychological condition of a social group that has endured for an extended period. This term is difficult to translate into Japanese since it differs from the English word "mentality," but it does not mean "national character."

Japanese industriousness resembles this "mentalité." In other words, it has persisted over a long period, but it is not unique to the Japanese people. If this point is not addressed early on, discussions of Japanese industriousness risk falling for the notion that the Japanese are racially superior. However, the fact that the Japanese were industrious for centuries cannot be denied. Foreigners who visited Japan during this period all expressed the same sentiment. Even today Japanese employees work in excess of 1,700 hours a year, more than people in most of the OECD countries. These working hours become even longer if overtime is included. Naturally, long working hours does not automatically mean industriousness. The degree of concentration toward the work during working hours must be considered, and efficiency – in other words, productivity – cannot be ignored. However, for the Japanese, it is also a fact that they are not forced to work long hours.

What the author is trying to say is that at some point the Japanese became industrious for some reason, and that eventually they will no longer be. The Japanese people are likely witnessing the end of a 400-year era of industriousness. Putting matters of the future aside, as a student of history, the author would first like to examine when, and why, the Japanese became industrious.

A. Hayami, *Japan's Industrious Revolution*, Studies in Economic History,
DOI 10.1007/978-4-431-55142-3_6

6.2 Industrious Revolution versus Industrial Revolution

Recently, even in European and American academic circles, the phrase "Industrious Revolution" has come into use as a historical concept. To give an example, the American economic historian Jan de Vries presented a lecture entitled "The Industrial Revolution and the Industrious Revolution" when he assumed the presidency of the Economic History Association (United States) – a lecture that was later published in the association's *Journal of Economic History* (de Vries 1994; see also de Vries 2008). Also, the television program *The Day the World Took Off*, produced by Windfall Films for England's Channel Four Television, was broadcast between May and July 2000 and received high reviews. This program went back through history in search of the roots of England's Industrial Revolution, but Alan Macfarlane, a professor of social anthropology at the University of Cambridge, stated that in situations where vast amounts of human labor are invested, such as Asian wet-paddy rice cultivation, by nature it is headed toward an "Industrious Revolution."[1]

The author, of this volume, is the one who coined the term "Industrious Revolution" (Hayami 1976).[2] Later, the author had conversations with the author's friends de Vries and Macfarlane and communicated the author's ideas with them. Judging from the ways in which they have used the term, they must have thought that it is not inaccurate to use the term in discussing their own issues. However, they do not necessarily use the term "Industrious Revolution" the same way that the author does. As it happens, the term has already started a journey of its own.

First, in de Vries' article, as seen in the title "The Industrial Revolution and the Industrious Revolution," the two concepts are not at odds with each other but, rather, in a society where commercialization (which can be restated as the creation of a market economy) progressed, machines and the steam which moved them were introduced, and the Industrial Revolution began. In other words, the Industrious Revolution and the Industrial Revolution are seen as a continuum and differ from the author's original idea.

Also, Macfarlane, in statements he made on the television program, used these terms in regards to peasants working in wet-rice agriculture in Asian farming villages (based on context, probably the farming villages in Nepal he continues to research). Naturally, he followed with the important statement that rice had a higher

[1] The subtitle was "The Roots of the Industrial Revolution," and it was a 50-minute television program of extraordinary quality broadcast every other week in 2000 for an eight-episode run. The text for this program was *The Day the World Took Off* by Sally and David Dugan (Macmillan 2000).

[2] Akira Hayami, "Joron: keizaishakai no seiritsu to sonotokushutu (Introduction: The Emergence of Economic Society and its Characteristics)." *Toyo Keizai Shinposha*. pp.3–18. This volume is the report of the 45th Socio-Economic History Society in June 1976, Waseda University, Tokyo. The author organized there a session "In Search of a New Image of Edo Period History" and gave the general presentation. There the author reported the "Industrious Revolution" as a character of agriculture in the Edo Period.

seed-to-yield ratio than wheat, and an even larger population could be supported with the same amount of land.

The author considers these two revolutions as opposing concepts with different directions, as seen in the title to this article. That aside, the author will discuss these ideas below.

6.3 From Livestock Power to Human Power: Changes in the Agricultural Production System in Tokugawa Japan

The author has conducted research on population and agriculture in the Nōbi region during the Edo Period. An extremely interesting fact the author discovered in this research is the changes to be discussed below. The largest daimyō in the Nōbi region was the Owari Domain, which constructed Nagoya Castle, and they surveyed the population, households, and livestock in the villages within their holdings in the 1670s and the 1820s. The survey in the 1670s was conducted by the domain itself, and the one in the 1820s was by one of their vassals. Although the one in the 1820s differs from the one in the 1670s in the sense that it was not an official survey, it does allow for comparisons of populations, households, and livestock. The total number of villages that have results from both surveys is 934: 725 in Owari and 209 in Mino (although it is not complete because the results from one district could not be obtained in the survey documents from the 1670s). The total population of these villages was 266,071 in Owari, and 77,315 in Mino. After 150 years, the populations were 332,258 and 112,298, respectively. The 8 districts in Owari all had increases, with the exception of one unclear district, and all 18 districts in Mino had increases. However, there were also areas that showed decreases at the village level. Of particular interest are the many villages around the castle town of Nagoya (population of approximately 100,000) that had population decreases, which could be seen as the result of the urban graveyard effect.[3]

There are these types of exceptions, but as stated earlier the region had population increases overall: approximately 25% in Owari, and approximately 45% in Mino. Considering the length of the 150-year period, this level of population increase was at an annual rate of 2–3‰ (per thousand), which compared to modern standards is not a large percentage. However, even increases at this level would be large if they continued over the long term, and in fact, in Tokugawa Japan, the Nōbi region was one region that had population increases.

[3] Prior to the general application of the fruits of modern industrial technology to urban life, cities, in particular large cities with concentrated populations, had a higher mortality rate than birth rate, so naturally the net population growth was negative. In order to maintain and increase an urban population, a large-scale population influx from surrounding rural area was necessary. This is called in Europe the "urban grave effect."

It is from these observations that the author acquired the concept of the Industrious Revolution. The Industrious Revolution does not anticipate the Industrial Revolution, nor does it simply point to labor-intensive Asian agriculture. More than anything, the Industrious Revolution was a method the peasants – who were the principal factor of production – selected as a response to the market economy in order to increase the yields. These motivations were precisely the necessary and sufficient conditions for the Industrious Revolution.

Also, it is not that the author said that pointing to labor-intensive rice agriculture. In other words, when that increased yield (Y), it was not an increase of capital (livestock = K), but a phenomenon brought forth by the increased amount of invested labor (L), another production element. In other words, regardless of the lowered K/L ratio, it points to cases where Y increases. The Industrial Revolution comes as an extension to increases in capital (K), but even if technological developments are possible as an extension of invested labor (L), it does not lead to an Industrial Revolution (Fig. 6.1). During the Edo Period, Japan was unable to achieve an Industrial Revolution under its own power, but as a result of its encounter with Europe and the United States, which had experienced the Industrial Revolution, it was imported to Japan. According to the author's conceptualization, the Industrious Revolution takes place when and only when there is a "motivation to increase Y."

6.4 Change in the Number of Livestock

In the two surveys conducted in the Owari Domain, in addition to the population, the number of livestock in each village was also surveyed. The livestock traditionally used for agriculture in Japan were horses in the east, oxen from central to western Japan, and horses again on the edge of western Japan. However, the Nōbi area was the westernmost of the areas in eastern Japan which used horses, but just over

Fig. 6.1 Industrious Revolution and Industrial Revolution

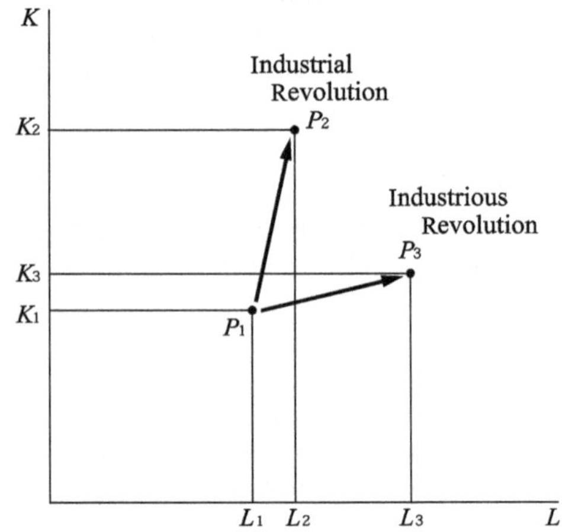

Table 6.1 Change in the number of households, population, and oxen/horses in the Owari Domain

	1670's	*1820*	Rate of Change
Number of Households	47,822	79,254	+ 65.7
Population	265,522	331,678	+ 249
Oxen/Horses	12,986	4,200	− 67.7

*The number of villages is not uniform since this table indicates changes in villages where comparisons are possible. This is an aggregateof approximately 700 villages.
**The figures for the 1670s are from "Records of villages in the Kambun period" (Kambun muramura oboegaki) and those for the 1820 figures from "Records of villages in Owari domain" (Gunson junkōki).

the mountains was a region which used oxen (Ōmi Province). Consequently, the number of horses recorded in the livestock surveys was overwhelmingly greater than that of oxen. However, the type of horses used in this region at this time is unclear. The native Japanese horses which remained on the western edge of western Japan were considerably smaller than European breeds imported to Japan during the Meiji Period, and could not possibly produce even one horsepower's worth of work. Nevertheless, they were stronger and swifter than oxen, and required more feed.

The survey conducted in the 1670s recorded 12,337 oxen and horses for 635 villages in the Owari Domain. This became 4,200 in 1820 – a decrease to one-third. The most conspicuous decreases were around Nagoya and the coastal flatlands, where the number was reduced to 20% of the initial level (see Table 6.1).

On the other hand, Mino did not show as much of a decrease as Owari, but it was still approximately 45% in the flatlands. The decrease was 78% in the mountainous areas. Thus, topographical differences can be seen in the decrease in the number of livestock, but when combined with population increases, the number of livestock per-capita drastically decreased everywhere.

In Owari, the number of livestock per thousand people went from 50 in the 1670s to 13 in the 1820s. In other words, the number decreased to approximately one-fourth. In Mino as well, the 65 in the flatlands of the 1670s were reduced to 21, or approximately to one-third, in 1820s. This major change resulted from the fact that the population increased while the number of livestock decreased. What does this drop in the K/L ratio mean? It goes without saying that the work that was performed by livestock was assumed by humans. Human power replaced livestock power.

The observations above are naturally phenomenon limited to the Nōbi region, and the situation in the other regions is unclear. Particularly in regions where oxen were the primary form of livestock, there is also the possibility that their numbers did not decrease since oxen were more effective than horses.[4] However, the decrease in the number of horses seen in the Nōbi region cannot be considered an independent phenomenon limited to just this region; the number of horses undoubtedly decreased at least in eastern Japan.

Normally, "modern development" in agriculture means that there is a greater investment of capital (K) in production, so the proportion held by labor (L), another production factor, decreases, and the yield (Y/L) per producer increases – in other

[4] Oxen were not used for food during the Edo Period, but their hides and bones were important materials for handicrafts.

words, labor productivity improves. Under this assumption, the phenomenon viewed in Tokugawa Japan was a change in the exact opposite direction. Under these changes, is it that labor productivity dropped and per-capita peasant income increased? Or did their income decrease – in other words, did they become impoverished?

Answering these questions is not easy. However, at the very least the peasants' living standards did not drop – rather, the reverse was seen: improvements in food, clothing and shelter. The apparent results of these improvements can be seen in prolonged life expectancies. In the case in the Suwa region of Shinano Province, the life expectancy at the end of the seventeenth century was 25 years, but it increased to 35 years at the beginning of the nineteenth century. In a society that did not have modern medicine or public health, reasons other than improved living standards cannot be found for the increases in life expectancy, and this would not have occurred in conditions of poverty.

Now, let us consider the effects of livestock on agriculture. Particularly Japan, which is based on wet-paddy rice cultivation, livestock would be the most effective during the spring plowing months. Pulverizing hardened soil while plowing it allows the soil to be used for cultivation up to a specific depth, which means vertically increasing the planted acreage. Deeper plowing increases soil productivity. The plows during the early Edo Period were small and unsuited to deep plowing. Therefore, spades and hoes which relied on human power were what made deep plowing possible.

The fertility of this land was increased by laying down compost made from livestock manure and undergrowth. In other words, this three-dimensionally increases the amount of soil used for crop cultivation. Thus far, livestock were highly effective for both plowing and producing fertilizer. Nonetheless, once the soil is prepared and water is drawn in, livestock are unnecessary for preparing the rice seedlings and then actually planting them. Water-filled fields required weeding and additional fertilization, but these tasks could largely be performed by hand, so there was no need to involve livestock.

After plowing in the spring, livestock were largely used not for agriculture. Fertilizer was obtained from communal village lands, forests, and common grasslands, and livestock was very effective when compost was primarily made by mixing cut grass and manure. Also, livestock were needed for hauling crops after the harvest.

Yet, during the Edo Period, fertilizer switched to that made from *sake* dregs and dried fish (particularly sardines and herring). Forests were cleared due to the increases in population, and due to these areas being used to cultivate the food and raw materials for human consumption; there were fewer and fewer areas where livestock feed could be obtained. Inevitably, raising livestock became a costly endeavor. This was replaced by the peasants purchasing fertilizer from merchants. In the parlance of the times, fertilizer was referred to as either *ryokuhi* (self-supplied "green" fertilizer) and *kimpi* (purchased "gold" fertilizer). The reliance on purchased fertilizer required a type of advance investment, making agriculture a type of family business in conjunction with market-directed production. Once they became business operations, the economic principle of maximum effect at minimum cost came into play. Livestock were inefficient and expensive to care for, so their value came down, diminishing the peasant's homestead.

This is eloquently expressed by the change in the K/L ratio in Nōbi. Ceramics-producing areas in the Nōbi region were the ones where the number of livestock decreased the least, as livestock were highly effective in transporting raw materials, fuel, and the products. Also, the rate of decrease was low in forested mountain areas. This is because the costs for keeping livestock were low. However, livestock practically disappeared from the flatlands areas, and even in cases where just a few remained, there were so few that it is inconceivable that they were used for agriculture.

6.5 Changes in Agricultural Methods and Household Composition

Due to this reduction in the number of livestock, peasants likely had to work longer and harder. There are no statistics as to the number of hours peasants worked in a day, or the number of days they worked in a year; much less likely is the chance of survival of any diaries kept over an extended period of time, or records of agricultural operations, that can be linked to the reduction in the number of livestock.

However, although in a different region, there is a place where it is possible to track major changes in the composition of peasant families. This is the Suwa region of Shinano Province, where it is possible to use historical documents to verify the process in which extended families – which were common at the end of the seventeenth century – broke down into stem or nuclear families (Hayami 2001, pp. 66–119). Several-generation family members had lived with many unmarried *ge'nin* in one roof. Their numbers were likely adjusted to meet the demand for labor during the farming season, and during the off-season, they either had no work, or just performed miscellaneous duties. It goes without saying that their productivity was low, and they gradually disappeared when factors for market production entered the farming villages in this region. Also, extended families broke down into stem or even nuclear families.

Why did this breakdown occur? Just like the decrease in the number of livestock in the Nōbi region, this was a result of the farming households choosing more efficient management methods. In a society like Japan's, which focuses on rice cultivation, rather than managing large-scale farmland using a large workforce, it was economically more efficient to manage small-scale farmland with a conjugal family. A custom emerged where farming families would share labor during the farming season. The peasants, whether they owned land or not, became an operational entity that relied on the power of family labor.

In the Suwa region of Shinano Province, the number of livestock per capita would have undoubtedly decreased with the changes in family structure, although there are no historical documents that attest to this. Raising livestock, and collecting and transporting fertilizer, was the work done by the *ge'nin* included in large households. Along with the changes in agricultural methods, the need to support large numbers of *ge'nin* disappeared. There is a strongly seasonal character to what is necessary and unnecessary in agricultural labor. If we take rice cultivation as an example, the farming season consists of the early spring plowing and planting, the early summer weeding, and the fall harvest, but the harvest is followed by the off-season. Therefore, a traditional labor force suited to the farming season and retained for life is inefficient because it does not contribute to production during the off-season and must be supported instead. Once the market-economic principle of minimum cost for maximum effect entered farming villages, these types of traditional peasant families were forced to disband and change to a structure where conjugal families formed the core of peasant households.

However, these changes did not occur overnight. Quite the opposite, these changes occurred over a long period of time, and by modern sensibilities, they spread slowly. When this process is observed using the average household size of each village as an indicator in the Suwa region of Shinano Province, we see that it started spreading outward concentrically from the castle town of Suwa. The average household size of one village did not fall below 4.5 people, but once this number was reached traditional farming methods completely vanished, marking the point where agricultural methods that relied on family labor based on "early modern" conjugal families were established. The Suwa District had a radius of 25 km, but it required approximately 120 years for the average household size in the entire district to reach 4.5 people. The propagation of this change was at the rate of 200 m per year.

As there are no other examples, there is no way to determine whether this was fast or slow. Of course, these changes were slow when compared with modern advanced communication technology-oriented societies. However, given the obvious fact that there was no means of modern communication, nor were there any laws or regulations issued mandating these changes, but only word-of-mouth dissemination among families or between villages, then we cannot judge that they were particularly slow.

In addition, to the peasants of the era – particularly those who took the lead with traditional agricultural methods – it is not difficult to imagine that there would have been hesitation or resistance to fundamentally changing agricultural methods. The shift that dismantled extended families which persisted for generations, and operations that used *ge'nin* for life and replaced them with one where conjugal families managed operations and tenant rent was collected, was not a simple accomplishment. Without a doubt, they likely decided to dismantle this system when they saw people close at hand who successfully made this shift, which in some cases may have required generations.

6.6 Conclusion of this Chapter

The Industrious Revolution was not religious in character whatsoever. In this regard, it differs from the "Protestant Spirit" found in Europe and the United States. Industriousness was transmitted via churches in Europe and the United States, but in Japan it was primarily done within families, from parent to child, and from child to grandchild.

In the farm manuals, a huge number of which were published in the Edo Period, industriousness was referred to as a virtue, but not as a religious belief. Also, the Meiji state made industriousness a national target, and even placed statues of Ninomiya Kinjirō – the boy from the Edo Period who supposedly studied while carrying firewood on his back – on the grounds of elementary schools nationwide as a symbol of diligence.

As modern-day Europe and the United States have secularized, the pathways for transmitting industriousness have weakened, and in Japan, the defeat in World War II served as an opportunity for criticisms of the government-run educational system to surface; and as family ties have become diluted, the means for transmitting industriousness have rapidly weakened. During the postwar period of high economic growth, a few generations worked ferociously in order to raise the economic standards which precipitously dropped due to Japan's defeat in the war, imparting the image of "Japanese industriousness" to the rest of the world. However, once these objectives were achieved and increasing criticisms were mounted against long working hours and being workaholics, a change in direction toward a welfare state became visible and the Japanese gradually lost any particular claim to industriousness. Here, Japanese "industriousness" has faded out of its 400-year long historical mission, and it is moving away from the stage. Now that Japan has become a society that has a low birthrate and is graying and is one of decreasing population, it will be interesting indeed to see just what choices Japan makes.[5]

---

[5] Limiting "population" to those with the highest incomes, thus the working-age population with the most demands (ages 15–64), the population peaked at 87.26 million in 1995 (69.4% of the overall population), and has entered a stage of decline.

Chapter 7
Economic Development in Early Modern Japan

7.1 Assessing "Early Modern" in Economic History of Japan

This chapter explores some of the author's research findings and their related issues, with special emphasis on economic development, during the "early modern" period (covering the eras of Oda Nobunaga, Toyotomi Hideyoshi, and the Tokugawa Shogunate, according to the standard periodization in Japanese history). The historical category of "early modern" is primarily a political one, and although one may expect some kind of correspondence between political change and economic change (or economic development) in history, it cannot be a perfect one. Here, the term "early modern" is used to cover a period, and economic development that is believed to have taken place in that period, prior to the Meiji Restoration after which "modernization" became a government-set national goal; and by adopting this definition, it should be realized, we do not need to assume that there was a discontinuity in terms of economic development between the "early modern" and "modern" periods. Also, it should not be taken to imply that the term "economic development" is defined as one similar to the course of industrialization in Western Europe, nor does it mean the concept of economic growth or economic development that is used in theoretical economics. If the concept were to be narrowly construed, whether or not early modern Japan really experienced economic development would be highly debatable. Here, the term economic development is taken to mean just the quantitative expansion of economic activity, its intensification, and its permeation into all strata of society.

Generally speaking, scholars who deal with the early modern economy of Japan have two choices: one is to assert its backwardness by focusing on pre-modern elements which may be discovered there, particularly in comparison with early modern Western Europe which began to modernize earlier, or conversely, to positively

A. Hayami, *Japan's Industrious Revolution*, Studies in Economic History,
DOI 10.1007/978-4-431-55142-3_7

assess this period as a preparatory phase leading to modernization in terms of commodity production and the circulation of currencies, both of which grew during the Edo Period. The first may be referred to as the pessimistic view and the second as the optimistic view. Scholars' choice has been closely linked to the actual situation of the Japanese economy and also to the scholars' perception of that situation. When they sense that Japan's capitalism is at risk, the pessimistic view tends to be stronger, but when its development is considered to be on-track, the optimistic view will be touted as a new interpretation. Therefore, it is no surprise that before the post-World War II period of high economic growth the pessimistic view was dominant, while it was after that period when the optimistic view emerged. In 1960 when the author published a survey article, "Trends in Postwar Japanese Socioeconomic Historical Research," it was difficult to find any work on the Edo Period that emphasized what would be called "economic development" and, in actuality, the vast majority of publications released up to that point assumed a pessimistic stance (otherwise, nothing more than tracing individual events). Therefore, the appearance of the optimistic viewpoint after the 1960s as described here should mostly be attributed to the Japanese economy transforming itself during that period of growth. Also, the influence of modern theories of development and growth played an important part. In this respect, it is worth mentioning that from 1971 onwards, a quantitative economic history (QEH) study group was formed, and they went a substantial way towards fusing economic history and economic development studies into one coherent area of research.

As is well known, one of the salient features of Japan's economic history research is the dominance of the Marxian view of history – or the stage-theoretic approach to economic development. According to this view, early modern Japan was a pre-modern, feudal society, a stage which is supposed for any country to have gone through. It was characterized as a period prior to factory industrialization established with the Industrial Revolution. It is also postulated that the period immediately before the Industrial Revolution was the age of "manufacture" in the Marxian sense. How the Meiji Restoration should be evaluated, whether it should be viewed as a bourgeoisie revolution, and whether late Edo-Period manufacturing had reached that stage of "manufacture" in terms of the organizational evolution of industry – those are the questions.

However, "economic development" as discussed in this chapter is not used in that stage-theoretic sense. Although the author does not deny that such an approach played a certain part in the historiography of early modern economic history, this chapter takes a very different approach. In the following sections, the author first gives a brief sketch of the author's view on early modern Japan, then will discuss several areas of interest. While the coverage of issues and literature is not comprehensive, the emphasis is on how to approach the interpretation of Japan's early modern economic history. Given the complicated nature of this period, it is absolutely necessary to be explicit about what angle the author will take.

7.2 Early Modern Economy and Society: Emergence of Economic Society

When a country industrializes, there are two choices: leave it to competition among private-sector companies and agents in the marketplace, or adopt a state-led planned economy. In Meiji Japan, as illustrated by the setting-up of government-run factories in the early years, the agent promoting industrialization was the government, but within a relatively short period of time, most of them were sold off to the private sector, and it is an indisputable fact that private-sector entrepreneurs became the principal actors. While the government–industry relations are often said to have remained close compared to those in Western European, Japan's industrialization itself was brought about by competition in the marketplace, which means that capitalism was chosen. The fact that a market-led path was an option for the country's industrialization is a crucially important proposition. As long as focus is solely on industrialization in the advanced capitalist countries, the market-led course is often regarded as something that must have been taken for granted. However, if we turn to other regions, we encounter many cases where capitalism was not an option. It was indeed other means that were taken for the promotion of industrialization. For the latter, there are cases in which socialist industrialization was the only option for a nation whose government was established under international circumstances of the twentieth century; historically, however, it is important to examine what made a capitalist path impossible in the past.

There were historical cases where capitalism was chosen for industrialization, but at the same time there existed cases where other means were taken. Then, what is the most fundamental, determining factor between those cases? The threshold, according to the author's view, was whether or not the country had reached a state which could be called an "economic society" immediately prior to the commencement of industrialization. Since much has already been said about the concept of "economic society," there is no need to repeat it here, but put very simply, it is a society where the people of a country, down to the common people, can act in an economic manner; in other words, it is a society where the economic value is independent from other forms of values, and people's action is based on the maximum benefit at minimal expense principle. When people's behavior is arranged along this line, a variety of economic mechanisms are established, which in turn regulate the activity of the people. In reality, of course, a completely "economic" society does not exist. Since people possess a multifaceted value system, even if what determines their thought and behavior is a facet of economic activity in the broadest sense, there usually remain even in the present, cases where economic judgments are outweighed by non-economic considerations. Further into history, economic valuation existed only in a subordinate form to other values, such as religious or political ones. This can also be seen from the history of economic doctrines. Economics became independent fairly late. As a science which by nature explores the principles of economic mechanisms, not just merely to describe economic facts, even in Western Europe its birth had to await the appearance of mercantile theories of the sixteenth and seventeenth centuries, or the eighteenth-century physiocrats, and finally Adam Smith's *Wealth of Nations* published in 1776. It is certain that economic principles came first, and the theory came into being in order to explain them.

For Japan seen from this viewpoint, it was the early modern period under Tokugawa rule that was crucial for an "economic" society to emerge. The Edo Period was by no means simply one of stagnation filled with exploitation. Rather, it was a society that experienced unprecedented internal transformations with the increased circulation of currencies and commodity production reaching to every corner of the country, giving birth, as noted earlier, to a scientific economic reasoning on the basis of observations of the reality. At the same time, this is not to say that Edo-Period Japan was a modern society. Far from it, politically it was without doubt a pre-modern society where the non-market relations of tribute and labor service existed between the ruling samurai and the ruled classes of merchants and peasants. In a number of spheres, therefore, political systems must have interfered with the free operation of economic activity and market principles. The traditional view of the Edo Period tended to emphasize excessively this aspect of political and social structures acting as an impediment to economic development. In addition, the eye-catching facts such as the so-called "national seclusion policy" and the long-term stagnation in population totals in the latter half of the period helped the pessimistic view gain weight. However, Edo-Period Japan, even with its lordship-*nengu* system, cannot be equated by any means with a "pure", feudal society in the sense that the term is understood in European history.

A few obvious facts will suffice to show that it was not. The samurai were separated, aside from two or three exceptions, from the peasantry under daimyō rule, which was also true for the shogunate's own territory. This meant that the samurai moved to the castle town, receiving *nengu* from the rural villages under the *kokudaka* system in the form of rice and, to a lesser extent, currency. A portion of the rice was directly consumed, but the remainder and the *nengu* received in currency were used for administrative expenses, on the one hand, and for the purchase of goods and services necessary for their lifestyle. A crowd of merchants and artisans, as well as service providers, surged to the early modern castle town in response to this cash expenditure. In other words, the emergence of the castle towns meant the appearance of a large, cash-using consumer group. Looked at in this light, Hideyoshi's policy, taken over by the Tokugawa shogunate, of separating the samurai from the peasantry had a tremendous impact: regardless of original intent, it abruptly created an economic dynamism in the stationary state. Although there were some differences in scale, over 200 castle towns were constructed nationwide. The beginning of the seventeenth century, therefore, was a period of unprecedented economic impact on the country's rural sector. Japan's early modern society made a completely different departure from that of Western European feudal society, which had to start with an extremely stagnant economy.

Furthermore, the alternate attendance system (*sankin kōtai*) is likely to have extended the local impact of both the samurai–peasant separation and the town construction onto a national scale. This system, for which approximately one-third of the daimyō's budgets were expended, gave birth to the metropolis of Edo, and "the pantry of the realm," i.e., Osaka which was responsible for supplying goods to Edo. The economic interaction of this sort was not just limited to the castle town and its surroundings, but it prepared a national market economy to emerge eventually, be it through the castle towns or otherwise.

It is true that the objectives behind the samurai–peasant separation policy, castle-town construction, and the alternate attendance system were not to aim for economic development in any shape or form. Rather, the shogunate's objective of the alternative attendance system is said to have been to reduce the wealth of daimyō. In fact, the shogunate and domainal governments frequently issued laws and ordinances, suggesting that they even tried to stem the tide of the growing commodity and currency economy at both national and local levels. Ordinances targeting the peasantry, such as those restricting crop plantings and ordering people to move back to their native land, were for no other purpose than to limit their production to *nengu* provision and self-sufficiency. These laws and systems, however, cannot be regarded as a source of evidence for the actual state of the economy without questioning the degree to which this official stance was effective.

Yet on the other hand, it is certainly not the case that the economic impact of those reforms have adequately been researched. The paucity of numerical data, in particular, makes quantitative analysis difficult. The following is thus a tentative attempt to provide a rough quantitative sketch of the samurai's tribute economy.

First, suppose that the *kokudaka* for all of Japan was 30 million *koku*, with the proportion that went to the shogunate and the *hatamoto* (bannermen) being one-fourth (7.5 million), and the daimyō taking the remaining three-fourths (22.5 million). This supposition is not too far from reality as figures for the eighteenth century onward with margins of error in the range of several percentage points. Then, it is assumed that the samurai took 50% of the *kokudaka* as *nengu*, and that 60% of that share was in rice and the rest in currency, making the samurai's income from the villages 1.5 million *ryō* in gold and 2.25 million *koku* in rice for the shogunate and *hatamoto*, and 4.5 million *ryō* in gold and 6.75 million *koku* in rice for the daimyō sector. The price of one *koku* of rice being one *ryō* in gold, the samurai's total income from the villages amounted to 3.75 *ryō* in the shogunate and *hatamoto* and 11.25 *ryō* in the daimyō sector. It is difficult to calculate the amount of tribute not from the villages, but if we assume that the samurais' non-rural income equaled 20% of their rural revenue in the shogunate and *hatamoto* and 10% in the daimyō sector, both in currency, then their cash income was 2.25 million and 5.6254 million *ryō*, respectively. Assuming further that while 40% of the rice income was directly consumed, the remainder was sold at the rate of one *koku* to one *ryō*, the cash earnings they received from the market was 1.35 million and 4.05 million respectively. Together with their non-rural earnings, their total cash income amounted to 3.6 million *ryō* for the shogunate sector and 9.675 million *ryō* for the daimyō sector.

On the other hand, expenditure estimates are entirely a matter of speculation. As it is likely that their entire income was spent, it is assumed that the shogunate spent 80% of the income and the daimyō 33.3% in Edo. This means that with the two sectors combined the annual expenditure of the government (including salaries for samurai civil servants) was 6.1 million *ryō* in cash a year in the metropolitan city of

Edo and 7.2 million *ryō* outside of Edo. All this is speculative and the calculation does not include debts. Nonetheless, it seems certain that this enormous "government expenditure" made the castle town of Edo into a metropolis with a total population that reached one million. The majority of the remaining expenditure is likely to have been spent in Kyoto and Osaka, whose populations were 400,000 and 500,000, respectively, and also in the other castle towns, thus keeping the level of urbanization high, including several with populations of at least 100,000. The above estimates are made on figures called *omote daka* (the official *kokudaka* determined and recognized by the shogunate at the beginning of the period), which means that the samurai's actual income and expenditure could have been much greater.

Given the circulation of currency in the Edo Period, approximately 20 to 30 million *ryō* (excluding copper coins), the weight of government expenditure and, in particular, the impact of the samurai's spending in Edo, should be self-evident. It is, therefore, very likely that such a forced creation of flows of currency and goods played an important role and, in fact, triggered transformations that turned Edo-Period Japan into an "economic" society.

7.3 Population, Prices and Wages

7.3.1 Population

This section presents a survey of findings on population, prices, and wages – an area where quantitative research has been under way. As mentioned in the previous section, the castle town construction and the introduction of the alternate attendance system acted as an initial push. The sudden emergence of demand for commodities in the cities must have been a major shock to the countryside which supplied almost all products. The attention of economic historians has so far been limited to research areas such as the establishment of village organization and the landlord-*nengu* system, for which documents survived, making more or less direct observation possible. Questions like the response of the supply-side to the impact created by this increased demand have never been asked, partly because data did not exist but partly because they lacked such perspectives. However, if we turn to the issue of changes in the structure of farm family and labor force and that of population growth, then we can demonstrate how great the transformations were. During this period, it is often said, "the large and complex farm family household (including non-lineal branch families and non-kin subordinate labor), which had been a dominant form in medieval times, dissolved and changed itself into a small household containing only one conjugal family unit." Under the current state of research, it is difficult to provide a sketch of this presumably countrywide change. But since the change began with the separation of the samurai from the peasantry and the construction of castle towns in the early seventeenth century, the changes in the family structure must have also been the rural response to that impact. As for the structural change in the labor force, there is evidence that "family farming" emerged in the sense that members of the stem family became the primary labor force. When busy, the stem-family household employed supplementary work hands, for whom a workforce of servants on a yearly (one-year in most cases) or seasonal contract, or casual workers on the daily basis, replaced the traditional group of hereditary subordinates (*fudai ge'nin*) or live-in servants on a longer-term contract. It is not difficult to detect here also that "economic" calculation was at work.

More evidence is available for population growth. According to the traditional view the national population in ca. 1600 was 18 million, which was a guestimate derived from a too-simplistic set of assumptions. The author's own calculation puts it at 12 million with a margin of ±2 million. Since the estimate based on the shogunate's 1721 survey was 30 million, it implies that there was a significant population increase in between – the population more than doubled during the seventeenth century.

Many case studies support this claim. The study utilizing the *shūmon aratamechō* for 38 villages in the Suwa region of Shinano Province confirms that the rate of population increase between 1671 and 1700 averaged 1% a year. This was accounted for by a high birth rate, but this high birth rate resulted from a combination of lower ages at marriage and higher marriage rates. Also, there was a significant decrease in the number of people who died unmarried, implying that non-inheriting children got married, formed branch families, and created families of their own. When there were no restrictions on the branching-out, the population must have increased. During the seventeenth century, there was room for the further extension of arable land; land use became more intensified; and urban growth absorbed a large number of the village population – all this meant that there was no need to resort to the practice of family limitation. Thus, the high rate of population increase continued.

Population growth is likely to have helped the aggregate demand to expand in a pre-industrial society where technological progress tended to be sluggish. It is therefore very likely that although self-sufficiency did not disappear overnight, seventeenth-century Japan was a period of growing demand.

Arable land also expanded in a manner similar to that of the population. Unlike pre-1600 *shoen* proprietors, the early modern daimyō were able to exert unilateral control over their domainal territories. Even in regions such as the Kantō and Osaka plains, where small domains were intertwined, large-scale flood control and irrigation projects were implemented by the shogunate, which enabled the conversion of fertile river deltas to a stable production base of the country. Also, small-scale land development was made by village communities or wealthier farmers in various parts of the country. As a result, seventeenth-century reclamation must have proceeded at a pace never seen before.

However, this kind of extension in the first half of the Edo Period came to a halt: the expansion of arable land reached a point where virtually all the cultivatable land was converted to farmland. The pace slowed down, and in the latter half of the Edo Period no reclamation became possible with the exception of coastal development in several areas. In addition, the frequency of cold summers in the eighteenth century gave a serious blow to agricultural production in Tōhoku and North Kantō, which is reflected in population trends in those regions. The population totals were on the decline until around 1840, so the peasants were forced to cut the number of children by resorting to infanticide and abortion. As far as the latter half of the Edo Period is concerned, economic development in these regions was halted. In the cases of the Yonezawa and Aizu Domains, for which we have data on population trends, the commoner population of the domains peaked in the early eighteenth century. Thereafter, it started to decrease and experienced a precipitous decline twice, in the Hōreki and Temmei Periods (the 1750s and the 1780s), reaching its trough at the end of the eighteenth century (for the population decline in northeast Japan, see Drixler 2013).

However, this eighteenth-century crisis did not affect other parts of the country. In southwestern Japan, the population continued to increase at a moderate – if not high – rate, in sharp contrast with Tōhoku and North Kantō. Indeed, these regions saw production continue to expand in the form of new second crops and farm family non-agricultural by-employments. According to the first national population survey taken by the shogunate in 1721, two groups of provinces in North Kantō (Kōzuke, Shimotsuke, and Hitachi) and in San'yō (six provinces other than Mimasaka) had approximately equal populations of 1.8 million each. At the 1846 survey, however, the former's population declined to 1.3 million while the latter increased to 2.3 million. Combining the populations of these two areas yields a total of 3.6 million – no net change. What is clear is that the use of the term "stagnation" for Japan is inappropriate, and hence that population trends should be discussed on a regional basis.

These examples suggest that we must be careful when considering the economy of early modern Japan. While there were regions where economic development took place, there existed regions that stagnated, or worse yet, fell into decline. Taking the total of both would produce stagnation, but this is a fallacy of aggregation. In a society where the national economy was yet to be developed, "stagnation" cannot be inferred from population trends alone.

What needs clarification is the fact that the population remained almost constant in regions generally considered most prosperous – South Kantō, the areas around Edo, and the Kinai, the areas around Kyoto and Osaka. According to early Meiji statistics, the two regions had conspicuously higher urban population ratios than others and were most advanced economically. Since it is likely that the conditions were similar in the latter half of the early modern period, the relationship between economic activity and population was different from what we would expect for areas where urbanization was at a high level. What the author has found here is a negative feedback function at work between pre-modern economic development and regional population change. The former led to a population concentration in the cities, but with high mortality and low fertility levels; the urban reproductive capacity in any pre-modern circumstances is likely to have been negative, so that a large number of migrants were needed from the surrounding countryside just to maintain the urban population. This is a mechanism that findings from the author's recent historical-demographic studies of towns and villages, although they are all case studies, are suggesting.

In the late 1830s, Japan once again experienced a major population decrease. Famine is said to have been the cause, but although there certainly occurred crop failures, deaths were caused by the spread of communicable diseases. According to the population survey for 1840, the population decrease which started in 1834 was countrywide, but Tōhoku, Hokuriku, and San'in were hardest hit. Also serious was a population decline in the cities with an 11% decrease in Osaka over a 2-year period. However, unlike the population decreases during the Temmei years (1780s), recovery was swift and in many cases the increase was maintained from the latter Tokugawa years into the Meiji Period. Particularly noticeable was the population up-turn in rural towns and villages in contrast to the large cities and castle towns where the population did not recover. What is suggested is a possibility that the traditional, urban-centered pattern of consumption-induced population change was beginning to shift to a new, rural-centered one.

Finally, recent research points to another fact: that the rural population of the eighteenth and early nineteenth centuries was far more mobile than previously thought (Hayami 2010). Tracing the events individual peasants born in a village of Mino Province underwent in life, 50% of males and 60% of females who reached the age of 11 left the village at least once. They went into service and approximately two-thirds of them, calculated by person-years, headed for cities and towns. The reason given on the document to these movements was "left temporarily for work," but approximately half of them did not return – some died in the place they were working, some got married, some moved their residence there, and some worked there for more than a couple of decades. It is not yet certain if this piece of evidence on high labor migration rates suggests the countrywide emergence of a labor market, but is a finding of considerable significance.

7.3.2 Prices and Wages

The Edo era was a time when the rise of markets for commodities and labor, and probably for capital as well, was under way. Recent studies in those research areas indicate how remarkable it was. Rice, a commodity traded in largest quantities throughout the period, was at the forefront of market growth. It was the *kuramai* that established a major supply route to the market since the daimyō collected it as *nengu* from the peasants. This involuntary nature of supply gave the market a considerable degree of stability. Harvest failure on a national scale was followed by soaring prices, and so was currency debasement. But in general, price fluctuations were kept within an acceptable range.

According to studies in the long-term trends of rice prices at various regional markets, it seems that there was a common fluctuation pattern with the Osaka market taking the lead. Also in the Osaka rice market there emerged the practice of *chōaimai* (on-the-book transaction), which eventually led to trading in futures. It is argued that the practices helped the market prices stabilize. However, the supremacy of the Osaka rice market declined towards the end of the period and its function as a central market was weakened. Given the aforementioned population decline in the metropolitan cities and castle towns, it suggests that government-involved economic activity declined in the later period of the Tokugawa shogunate. It is likely that the Osaka market was outcompeted by the rise of the local economies, particularly those in southwestern provinces.

When several commodity price data series are available for the long-run, changes in the relative price indices may be examined. The Osaka wholesale prices can be classified into four categories: food crops, industrial crops, processed foodstuffs, and non-foodstuff processed goods. Looking at the relative changes in each category, the following observations can be made (Shimbo 1978). First, in the eighteenth century, the prices of agricultural products for food and agricultural raw materials for industry were on the decline; for example, the prices of rice, soybeans, and wheat remained low compared with those of rapeseed and ginned cotton. Behind such trends was the increased industrial demand for raw materials, in other words, the growth of the processing sector. The rise in their relative prices must have acted as a major stimulus to the expansion of production in that kind of commercial agriculture. In the following period of sustained price rise from the 1820s to the end of the 1850s, the relative prices of non-foodstuff processed goods tended to rise, which cannot be explained by the price elasticity of demand. An increase in the effective demand for those products is likely to have been the factor accounting for the upward trend in their relative prices in the first half of the nineteenth century. The up-turn of the population trend from the beginning of the century and the increase in per-capita income can be interpreted as indicating an increase in the aggregate demand for non-foodstuff processed goods in this period, suggesting that any changes in the relative prices are useful in interpreting changes in economic structure.

At the same time, a lead and lag analysis of commodity prices is also useful in deciphering changing economic as well as price structures. For example, the price rise in the Temmei years (1780s) first showed up in prices of rice and industrial raw materials, and with a one-year lag in prices of food crops and non-foodstuff processed goods, and finally, in those of processed foodstuffs. While the price rise of rice is what we would expect in a period like the Temmei famine, it should have been followed by a rise in the prices of food crops other than rice, but in fact this did not happen. This shows that the rise in prices in that period were not simply due to a supply-side anomaly such as famine, but were also accompanied by changes in the demand for individual product categories.

Recently, several studies have been published on time-series of factor prices such as those of lending, interest rates, and any other indicators of the money market. Moreover, those of real wages, deflated with long-term price indices, are also available. Since those markets were never perfect, it is desirable to compare one with another within one geographical area; and it is now possible to do as far as the Kinai region is concerned. From the two series of wages for carpenters and agricultural day laborers in a villages in western Settsu Province, we know that a substantial increase in real wages and a rapid contraction of the wage differential took place between the 1730s and the early 1770s. Both slowed down noticeably in the period between the late 1770s and the early 1820s, followed by a decrease in the level of real wages with creeping inflation from the 1820s onwards (Saito 1976).

7.4 Economic Policies and Economic Models

Although early modern Japan took a political structure known as the *bakuhan* system with the shogunate assuming a superior position over daimyō, in reality much of its internal affairs was left to the domain. Thus the integration of emerged markets proceeded and so did the national economy. However, it was extremely difficult for even the shogunate to implement macro-economic policies. In addition, despite the progress of "economic" society, their official ideology of Confucianism prevented them from implementing coherent policies for development. The so-called Three Great Reforms – in the Kyōho, Kansei, and Tempō Periods (the 1730s, 1790s and 1830s, respectively) – were polices that conservative factions of the shogunate tried to counterbalance the progressing forces of economic activity. Among these policies, those of Tanuma's are noteworthy, but even his reform plans were not always expansionist. Nor was it possible for individual domains across the country to do anything to synchronize their policies with the expansionist or austerity policies of the shogunate. While austerity measures were being taken under the Kyōho reforms by shogun Yoshimune, Lord Tokugawa Muneharu – daimyō of Owari, one of the three major branch families of the House of Tokugawa – took a rather expansionist stance. Foreign trade and coinage were areas the shogunate monopolized, but even these monopolistic rights were not absolute. For foreign trade, the trade with the Dutch and Chinese in Nagasaki were certainly brought under the shogunate's control, but they were unable to regulate Tsushima's trade with the Koreans or that of the Satsuma with the Ryukyus. As for currency, while the minting of official gold and silver currencies was under control by the shogunate, the supply of paper money (*hansatsu*) was not; from the Kyōho years on, the domainal government was in reality allowed to issue the domainal notes by making notification to the shogunate. In other words, it was impossible for the central government to control the total amount of money in circulation.

It is worth noting here that some form of industry promotion policies emerged for specific products and trades among senior-level samurai bureaucrats, especially in the domainal governments. Many historians have tended to talk of those policies negatively, since the daimyō government often monopolized the transactions within the domainal economy. This ill effect certainly cannot be ignored. But considering the early modern daimyō under strong influences of anti-mercantile doctrines, the fact that their governments went for introducing industry-promotion policies carries weight; they established trade bureaus whose primary function was to supply working capital to buy up commodities for "export" to the metropolitan markets. It is not difficult to see some kind of continuity with the Meiji government's development policies. It is true that most of these policies were a failure, and that their initial objective was to ease the domain's financial difficulties. What is more significant is the emergence of trade and finance bureaucrats who took the lead in formulating those plans, and it is not unlikely that the accumulated stock of their know-how and experience formed a legacy that was succeeded by the Meiji government after the collapse of the *bakuhan* system.

If we accept that the national economy was created under Tokugawa rule, one may venture to construct a model of the early modern macro-economy. Two studies have so far been published which took up this challenge. However, since there is virtually no quantitative data on output of the nation, any model based on a national accounting framework would, if conceivable, remain unverifiable forever. Model building could be based on meticulous quantitative analysis of existing data, or if the data does not permit, on an accumulation of qualitative historical facts, but in reality neither is possible. One method that might work is to estimate an agricultural production function first, to convert its results into a dynamic formula, and then to check what changes in production factors such as population, capital, and arable land would produce; and second, to examine how the relationship between output and technology would change by a change in the ratio of one production factor to another. The results of such an "experiment" do lend support to the course of economic development suggested above for early modern Japan.

However, several questions remain for this kind of model building in relation to early modern Japan's economic development. Given the economic decline of the eighteenth century on that, as noted earlier, the Tōhoku region suffered, a two-region model may be suggested: a region where output growth outweighed population increases (such as the Kinai region), and another region where the opposite occurred (such as the Tōhoku region). However, this model too would remain a working hypothesis where statistics on output or income are lacking.

Of course, such an attempt is significant in its own right, particularly when it enables us to put individually derived facts about factors of production such as population and price changes in order to account for broad tendencies. In this sense, results of such attempts will be discussed widely in the future.

On the other hand, this methodology will be far more effective if the analysis is limited to data derived from a single region. The *Bōchō fūdo chūshinan*, the exemplar of an economic and social survey conducted for a single domainal territory of Suō and Nagato Provinces, the western-most domain of Chōshū, provides us with statistical information on production factors and income (with non-agricultural earnings), and hence enables us to estimate production and consumption functions, and also a simplified version of a input–output table. Findings from the late Shunsaku Nishikawa's valuable studies brought about numerous discoveries ranging from the issue of how factors of production were combined to that of peasant income structure in this region of the 1840s. For example, the proportion of non-agricultural income in peasant household income is confirmed, which strongly suggests that the true rate of *nengu* must have been lower than previously assumed. What is suggested is a possibility that a favorable spiral was already prepared for modern economic growth, namely: creation of surplus → formation of capital → technological progress → increase in per capita output → further creation of surplus.

There are some more research findings concerning early modern economic development. However, the overview of the literature makes it clear that surprisingly little has been done to clarify conditions of production in the period in question. For early modern Japan, the fundamental issues of levels and growth of agricultural and handicraft productivity still remain unresolved. As stated at the very beginning, research has been concentrated on production organizations, land systems, and other related topics due primarily to the paucity of numerical data. Without knowledge about productivity and its increase, it is rather hazardous to talk about "economic development" as if it had been taking place. If evidence in the form of countrywide or cross-regional data is not readily available, even an accumulation of individual case studies would help us explore the issue in a more coherent manner.

Chapter 8
Conclusion: Historical Reflections on Japan's Industrialization

8.1 The Significance of the Edo Period for the Birth of Modern Japan

The discussions in the previous chapters make it clear that during the Edo Period it is possible to find preparatory signs of modern society and hence a historical continuity. However, the Edo Period was not a modern society. What triggered the transformations was the collection by the samurai of *nengu* from the peasantry, and this was one type of revenue economy (Hicks 1969, pp. 22–24). In other words, it was an economy where the movement of goods and currency arose because of differences in status: people with political authority imposed *nengu* obligations on the ruled. As long as this existed, the Edo Period was not a modern society. Peasants' *nengu* obligation was substantially different from our modern tax payment.

In almost all other aspects of economic life in the Edo Period, the transactions of goods and currency were conducted or came to be conducted "economically," but between the overlord and the peasantry the relationship remained ultra-economic. The land tax reform that immediately followed the Meiji Restoration was a task to bring this relationship formally into a modern taxation system. On the other hand, the *nengu* peasants had to pay under Tokugawa rule was also definitively different from the *shōen nengu* of pre-1600 eras in several respects, and it also cannot simply be considered oppressive. First of all, the *nengu* was not directed entirely to the personal consumption of the samurai, a significant portion was returned to the peasants in the form of governmental expenses. Therefore, the Edo-Period *nengu* should probably be regarded as having both the elements of both tax and rent. The land tax reform removed the element of "rent," so it was not a newly created land tax, but a *reform*. Second, under the *nengu* system it was the amount of the tax that was fixed. A cadastral survey was supposedly taken periodically and, in early years, several daimyō governments did another survey. But from about 1700 on, the amount became fixed without a fresh survey of yields, thus creating a disparity with

A. Hayami, *Japan's Industrious Revolution*, Studies in Economic History,
DOI 10.1007/978-4-431-55142-3_8

increased yields. The number of varieties of cultivated crops also increased, and advancement was made in production technology, so the fixed amount of *nengu* without a cadastral survey meant a decline in the *nengu*-output ratio.

Thus, characterizing the Edo-Period *nengu* system with heavy taxation as a form of exploitation prevents us to have an accurate understanding, and at the very least, it should be distinguished from *shōen nengu*. Caution is required when quantitative measures are used to determine if the *nengu* was oppressive. It is true that tax payments were burdensome for the class of smallholders since it was not progressive, like a modern-day income tax. For this sort of calculation, however, the value of services should be taken into account. Even if the tax rate is small, *nengu* with zero return should be regarded as "oppressive." Conversely, the high tax burdens in welfare states should not be considered "oppressive." With these points taken into consideration, it is difficult to call the *nengu* obligations oppressive so as to completely destroy the lives of the peasants. In the government surveys conducted during the early Meiji land tax revisions, the *nengu* was set at thirty percent of the yield, but this estimate did not include off-season and second crops; it is likely that the actual level was much lower.

However, this does not imply that every peasant had light *nengu* burdens. Aside from the principal *nengu*, the peasants had to pay additional *nengu* as well as village dues (*murairiyō*). For villages along the official highways, providing porters and horses (*sukegō*) to official travelers was a considerable burden. During an era when people primarily depended on human power and horses for overland transport, the *sukegō* services were unbearable for the peasants especially during the farming season. This is clear also from the fact that the *sukegō* system was frequently the cause of riots. Wages were paid for the services, at times this served as a form of additional cash income when there was no work, but for villages of the Kantō region – where all five of the major highways met – the system was particularly burdensome.

For tenant farmers a major burden was rent payment. Landlords' bargaining power rose with the declining land-man ratio, so did rent levels. The amount of the tenant rents varied across regions, but in the surveys conducted by the Meiji government, it is said to have been approximately one-third of the yield. This was a considerable amount, and combined with the *nengu*, the tenant farmer's share was only one-third.

Therefore, the peasants were by no means wealthy. By modern standards they were poor. Yet, it should be clear that their material living standards improved, and their social standing also greatly improved compared to the situation at the beginning of the period.

The largest issue for the peasantry under a very intensive farming system was the amount of physically demanding and time-intensive labor invested in small plots of land. Not one inch of land went to waste, management was meticulous, and peasants had to work as a family from morning until evening to reap a harvest. In a sense, this intensive use of labor, the price of freedom from their subordinate status, was one of the salient features of Japanese agriculture. As such, it had a strong influence on the Japanese view of work, or moral discourse according to which hard work was a virtue. And this seems to have played an extremely large role in the initial stages of industrialization. It is often said that in Western Europe, the "Protestant ethic and the spirit of capitalism" had an important relationship to, and played a role in, its modernization. In Japan, it was the ethos of hard work. It was a moral, not a religious discourse, which was passed down within the family, from parent to child, and from child to grandchild. In other words, the stem family system (almost universal in Japan) was the channel for its transmission.

Now we examine the age of "manufacture" – or "proto-industrialization" according to a recent terminology. Industrial production increased during the Edo Period, especially in textiles and food processing, but there existed several fundamental shortcomings. The first is the problem with energy sources. Among the pre-industrial energy sources such as human, animal, wind, and hydropower, traditional Japanese industry used human power and, to a much lesser extent, hydropower: there was a kind of supply bottleneck. While there took place innovations and, hence, some improvement in efficiency in the areas of weaving, spinning and agricultural devices, the efficient use of energy sources lagged far behind Western Europe of the same period. This has some bearing on the underdevelopment of metalworking and machinery, which did not go beyond the stage of simple hand-manufactured devices, mostly made of wood, although some of those handmade goods were so minute and delicate that they were often rated highly for their artistic value. The generally upward trend in the relative prices of manufactured goods may be accounted for by this.

As a result, Japan is said to have not experienced the age of "manufacture" as one of the successive stages of capitalism. It is true that, toward the end of the period, there emerged a kind of centralized workshop in some local textile districts where, for example, looms were installed and weavers employed. However, in terms of fixed capital formation that remained in infancy. People did not have the concept of "capital" in the true sense; what they had instead was simply that of "working or circulating capital."

It is important to reiterate that agriculture and handicrafts did not follow a path of productivity growth, which led eventually to the introduction of modern machinery and other fixed assets of capital. A significant proportion of handicraft products were produced by peasants in their home in the form of by-employment, and made their way to the consumers market via multiple layers of distribution. As opposed to the production process, development was made in the distribution process: progress was made in wholesale networking and credit arrangements. Those must have functioned as favorable conditions for industrialization, but not in and of themselves the formation of agents who carried out industrialization.

Probably we may argue that the experience of Edo-Period Japan formed the conditions that enabled a relatively smooth adaptation of industrialism when the nation introduced it from abroad. Market-oriented production and money-using transactions, both of which spread to the ordinary masses, made people behave "economically." Then, this gave the people the desire to improve their living standards, which was linked to hard work. The peasants' standard of living rose steadily (although at a snail's pace compared by modern standards), so it is likely that they knew the significance of these changes that were taking place around them. Poverty and economic adversity could be overcome as long as it was compensated for by hard work. The lack of religious impediments also helped, but it was probably they who might have chosen amoral means to reduce population pressures for the fear of a decline in the standard of living more than anything else. It was precisely this attitude toward their lives that became the legacy of the Edo Period.

8.2 The Seigneurial System

On the other hand, no entrepreneurs came forward to carry out industrialization. Why?

First, unlike in Western Europe, neither "bourgeoisie" nor "civil society" rose in Japan. There is evidence that cities in the sixteenth-century Kinai were autonomous in the sense that their citizens were free from the overlord's control; but in the process of unification under Oda Nobunaga, Toyotomi Hideyoshi, and the Tokugawa shogunate these cities were brought under their control. As for cities and towns which were born under their rule, most of them were castle towns, i.e., settlements planned and built by the ruling samurai, in which they occupied a large, central area. Therefore, merchants of the castle town were first and foremost "official or privileged merchants" whose primary function was to meet the official needs in return for protection they received from the lord. The lord–merchant relationship was so deep that they were unable to act against the lord's will. Consequently, while they were unmistakably city dwellers, they were unable to act as "citizens" like their counterparts in Western Europe. What the city dwellers could do instead was to take advantage of the lord's financial predicament and gnaw away at the domain's wealth. Japan was not in a position to follow a path that would repudiate the *bakuhan* system.

Another factor is that the expansion of the new Tokugawa state structure known as the *bakuhan* system was premised on a certain level of institutional flexibility, which if conditions permitted would bring forth economic development. In the case of Western Europe, the feudal system was built on the premise that economic conditions were extremely unfavorable, thus exhibiting a kind of structural rigidity incompatible with economic development. Therefore, it is safe to say that those who shouldered economic development strongly desired the abolition of feudalism. Yet, Japan's *bakuhan* system was flexibly structured and thus absorbed and accepted a certain degree of economic development. Therefore, economic development and the seigneurial system were not completely at odds with one another. At any rate, when Western Europe abolished their seigneurial system – be it in England or in France – there was a great deal of bloodshed. In contrast, the Meiji Restoration was followed by the daimyō relinquishing their rights without a drop of bloodshed. Therefore, we must take this flexibility adequately into consideration. It is misguided to ask if it was a bourgeois revolution.

8.3 Production Technology

The second point that should be stressed is that in Japan production technology was labor-intensive and developed in the direction of saving capital, which was contradictory to the nature of industrialization. Industrialization is characterized by the introduction of new energy sources and new production technologies, but overall it is a means to attaining increased productivity per worker, or more precisely, increased productivity per unit of labor. This is clear for England, where industrialization took off first and spontaneously. There, after the introduction of agricultural technology using a large number of livestock and large-scale, heavy plows, labor productivity increased. There may have also been economies of scale operating. The consequence was a spread of unemployment in the countryside, suggesting that the direction of technological development was of great significance.

An increase in scale meant a further investment in production technology, and here emerged a new class of entrepreneurs – the very agent of industrialization – who linked the use of new technology and energy sources to capital deepening in combination of wage labor. In Japan, this type of entrepreneur did not appear as a mass in the Edo Period. The technological system was not one that allowed economies of scale to operate; rather, it was one constantly threatened by the law of diminishing returns. In agriculture in particular, the size of operation never increased. Land was leased out to peasants by the landlord who collected a handsome amount of revenue.

8.4 Population Pressure

The third point is the balance between population and resources, which was not conducive to industrialization in Japan. In the seventeenth century when the large and complex farm family household dissolved into a number of small households, checks on population increase were removed, and nuptiality and fertility increased, followed by a population explosion. The resultant improvement in living standards lowered the mortality rate and extended life expectancy. As the population came close to its limit, farmland and other resources could no longer keep up. While intensive agricultural technology was extending the acceptable limit, or while the urban capacity of population absorption was high, an increase in population may have not been a problem, but once this limit was exceeded, a state of overpopulation set in. Even when the population stopped growing, it exerted a great deal of pressure, which meant that labor could be obtained for bare-minimum subsistence wages. The conditions were favorable for the development of handicrafts and the gardening type of farming that required manual labor. However, this was a situation extremely unfavorable for labor productivity growth, i.e., capital-intensive industrialization. Population pressure was particularly high in northeastern Japan, where environmental conditions worsened and a type of agrarian crisis prevailed in the region from the end of the eighteenth century.

8.5 The Limitation of Market Growth

Finally, markets were virtually all domestic. In the first half of the period in question, the expansion of domestic markets extended production frontiers, whereas in the latter half of the period the expansion was restricted only in certain regions. But the pace of expansion slowed down in those regions. In this situation the societal demand for increased productivity was no longer strong. Therefore, it was after the opening of the Treaty ports when a second population expansion and market expansion led the way toward increased productivity.

8.6 Obstacles to the Industrial Breakthrough

Because these four factors worked in unison, internally the agents willing to carry out industrialization did not come forward. Inevitably, therefore, Japanese industrialization required an external shock. In the mid-nineteenth century, it was the encounter with the West, whose economic and military power was markedly different from Japan's, and the decision by Japanese political leaders to imitate the Western powers, that sparked the process of industrialization. Thus, the "agents" of industrialization were not private-sector entrepreneurs; it was state-led, at least in the initial stages of the process.

However, this was not unique to Japan; the industrialization effort was state-led in many other countries. Whatever the case may have been in England, the government played an extremely large role in major continental European countries, and even in America in its early stages. In the English case, the industrial breakthrough took place in textiles in the late eighteenth century and in the nineteenth a chain-reaction of innovations changed iron making and transportation, but the government was never involved. Yet, the other countries faced the situation of English supremacy and competitiveness, against which the governments had to take some sort of action. The best-known example of this is German protectionism. In other words, protective tariffs, subsidies, and even state-run model factories were used to protect domestic industries and promote new ones for the purpose of economic development. The scope of government intervention in industrialization differed by country, but in most cases this was a common feature in countries that trailed behind the advanced nations in terms of industrialization.

By using capital supply as a criterion, Gerschenkron has presented a model where in the most advanced nations, capital was provided by the "factory" (namely, plowed-back); in the case of follower countries, it was provided by the "bank" (namely, financial institutions outside the industry); and in the underdeveloped countries, the "state" acted as a substitute. According to this model, governmental intervention in industrialization is not a feature exclusive to Japan. Moreover, it suggests that the lack of entrepreneurial talent may well have been substituted by an appropriate provision of capital. What was important is the response to the external shock, and the ability to direct this toward the country's own goal of industrialization in order to make up for the absence of the "agents" and other conditions for industrialization. Of course, the degree to which they were absent or unmet varied from country to country, but this type of thinking provides an answer to the question of whether industrialization is possible. Where capitalism was the sole means to industrialization, or where the experience of capitalism was historically inevitable, this question is never raised. However, it should be clear that industrialization through non-capitalist means was possible while capitalism was not always "inevitable." That being the case, it is important to ask whether Japan had that option despite a different set of conditions the country had achieved. Most economic historians thus far have not raised the question in that manner. The two systems of economic development presented in Chapter 1 (Fig. 1.2) are relevant in this context.

While the "conditions" were largely met in Japan, the factors that made "agent"-formation noticeably difficult became a heavy burden for the development of capitalism. Moreover, by the time the government launched a modernization program, the gap with the West had become apparent – the country was even behind the second group of industrializers on the European continent. However, considering the tremendous difficulties the developing countries have today, which are so great that a socialist path has emerged as one of the options before them, Japan may well have been the last nation to have capitalism as an option.

In this regard, Japanese industrialization had a number of features. The first is that it had to be "rapid." During the Meiji years, "catch up with the West" became the national slogan and the nation's ultimate goal. As a result, Japan's modernization was lopsided, and the cheapest and swiftest methods were chosen. It has been frequently observed that while growth was rapid in production and other areas in which immediate profits were possible, Japan lagged behind in other areas. Infrastructural development also took a back seat. Even today it is plagued with numerous discomforts and inconveniences, for which we are paying the price. The second is that Japan embarked on modernization in the age of the imperialist race for colonial expansion. Under such circumstances, Japan joined the race by building a military oversized for the country's economic foundation, which was eventually used to colonize the neighboring countries. The national wealth Japan poured into its military build-up reached an enormous level. Since this produced no results, military might was attained primarily at the sacrifice of people's standard of living. It was after the last World War when Japan was brought back on track, but before that period much of the country's national wealth was held in the form of battleships and fighter planes.

8.7 The Government

The third feature is the collusive government–business relationships. In the early Meiji Period, prior to the emergence of private-sector entrepreneurs, the government was the agent. The government-run factory is the most direct expression of this. From the mid-1880s on, the private-sector entrepreneurs appeared in textiles and railways, but they, too, received state protection and their relationship with the government was closer than in the West. Continental European countries and the United States, after an initial, state-led phase, transformed themselves to liberal capitalism, and the government's role in industrialization became indirect. This situation continued until the government once again became actively involved in promoting industrialization in the period after the Great Depression (Keynesian economics was established in this context). In Japan, the interval between the two periods of state intervention was extremely short (corresponding to a decade or so known as the period of Taishō Democracy in Japanese political history). Together with the aforementioned immaturity of the "bourgeoisie," the state has almost always been interventionist in the industrialization process since the early Meiji years until today. Even when the private sector was the driving force of economic progress, the government tended to act in the interests of the business corporations. Both government guidance and dependence on the government has been one of the pillars of the "Japanese style" of capitalism, distinctly different from the Western style – more precisely, the Anglo-American style.

The fourth feature is the spread of the family system, which very strongly penetrated into the other aspects of Japanese social life during the Edo Period. Furthermore, the family system was compatible with all other organizations, i.e., the state, business corporations, and unions. In contrast with the West, where individualism became the spiritual pillar of modern society, the reverse was true in Japan, where the family was the societal anchor. This may appear strange at first glance, but in fact, the Japanese family system was not shattered by industrialization; instead it was kept intact and has often been mobilized until recent years, with some change only in very recent years. The family system was introduced to, and functioned between, the state and the people, the corporations and employees, and all other groups of society. As a result, the entire social fabric takes the form of the so-called vertical society. Aspects of this vertical structure has sometimes been condemned or compared with that in the West. While it is unlikely that this structure would be sustainable in the future, this family structure may well have functioned as a "substitute" for what Western individualism did for modernization and industrialization.

Because of this familial element in the business corporation, a *Gesellschaft* (association), its employees become members of a *Gemeinschaft* (community), who work by putting aside their individual existence for the benefit of the corporation. Lifetime employment, seniority-based wage payment and company-unionism are all truly Japanese characteristics brought forth from the family system. By this means, poorly capitalized corporations in the early stages of development were able to safely grow up.

Therefore, unlike in other circumstances, the family system did not become an obstacle to industrialization – at least this was the case until very recently. If any late-comer country had had to wait for an individualist or civic social order emerging as a "condition" for industrialization, Japan's industrialization would have been delayed even further, or would have been forced to take a different path. On the other hand, as capitalism developed further, and economic growth continued, the demand for civic freedom and individualistic lifestyles would increase, and the traditional family system would thus be regarded as an obstacle. Several changes that occurred after World War II attest to the fact that a shift in that direction did occur. Modern Japan is confronted with the choice of whether or not it is possible to dismiss one system and shift to another without impeding economic development.

Japanese capitalism had numerous weaknesses and characteristics, so it was frequently besieged by peril. During the Great Depression of the 1930s, and the period immediately after World War II, doubts spread regarding the recovery of development. Dangers to this type of capitalism may in some aspects be explained by reference to economic fluctuations inherent to capitalism itself, and are not an exception as an advanced capitalist nation, but in the Japanese case the foundation on which it was established was relatively frail, so that the impact of those fluctuations was felt all the more strongly.

The experience of the Edo Period constituted several major conditions for Japan's industrialization. This observation can be made for non-economic aspects as well – for example, in the area of intellectual history, a similar account has been made on the evolution of rational thought. While it is undoubtedly true that Edo-Period Japan was atypical as a feudal society, it was a variation of "decentralized" society in the broadest sense of the term. It is probably safe, then, to say that Japan took a path to industrialization – namely, the path that went through the stage of "decentralized" society and that of "economic" society leading to capitalism.

8.8 Summary

At the end of the sixteenth century, an "economic" society had emerged in the Kinai and its surroundings; in the seventeenth century it spread virtually nationwide with the establishment of a new type of seigneurial system and its associated systems of landholding and taxation. The whole system was characterized by the adoption of a *kokudaka* system based on cadastral surveys. But as the samurai were separated from the peasantry, castle towns constructed, and consumption centers created from above, so was urban growth spreading across the country: urbanization that had been taking place in the Kinai region became nationwide, making an impact on the nation's countryside. In addition, since the Tokugawa shogunate introduced the alternate attendance system, Edo's population increased to one million – a sudden rise of a mass consumers' market, while Osaka established itself as a supply base of consumers' goods to Edo and other cities. A national economy was born.

On the other hand, the *nengu* to the overlord was paid in rice and currency, which means that rice had to be converted into currency. Thus goods, services, and currency circulated between the samurai, merchants, and peasants. The use of currency spread to people across Japan, giving incentives to the peasants' economic action, which in turn enabled the peasants to select optimal production methods and intensified farming by using family labor.

During the Edo Period, the measurable indices of population, arable land, and output increased at different rates. It is noticeable that the yield per unit of land was on the increase, showing that the manner of land management changed. Maintaining soil fertility was of utmost importance, while that of self-supplied fertilizers decreased, which implies that the peasants relied more on purchased fertilizers.

The impact of all this was felt in all areas of peasant life. The family became the source of labor, as the household consisted only of those directly related to the head. As a result, nuptiality increased and fertility rose, increasing the size of the population; a decrease in mortality and an increase in the average lifespan were accompanied by rising living standards. Much of this population expansion was absorbed by cities, but in the countryside, as long as land clearing and intensive farming developed, the population kept increasing right up to its limit.

Agricultural operations came to require more cash as the nature of fertilizer changed: the peasants began to buy fast-acting fertilizers (such as dried fish and oil cakes). This in turn made plowing deeper and weeding more frequent, compelling them to work long hours, but in the end this type of labor was optimal for family farming. The idea that hard work was a virtue became a family ethos, which was passed down within the stem family.

However, this spread of an "economically" minded society did not mean that a dynamic leading to industrialization was ready at the end of the Edo regime. The formation of "agents" was delayed; no internal forces led the way to political and social reforms from below. On the economic side, technological progress was in the direction of labor intensification, not capital intensification; there were supply bottlenecks derived from energy constraints as well as market constraints due to national isolation. For the startup, therefore, an external shock was needed. All this means is that adequate preparation was made in the Edo Period – adequate for the country to promptly respond to the external stimuli and to follow the capitalist path in order to achieve industrialization under late nineteenth- and twentieth-century circumstances.

References

Boxer CR (1951) The Christian century in Japan, 1549–1650. University of California Press, Berkeley

de Vries J (1994) The industrial revolution and the industrious revolution. J Econ Hist 54(2):249–270

de Vries J (2008) The industrious revolution: consumer behavior and the household economy, 1650 to the present. Cambridge University Press, New York

Drixler F (2013) Infanticide and population growth in Eastern Japan, 1660–1950. University of California Press, Oakland

Dugan S, Dugan D (2000) The day the world took off: The roots of the industrial revolution. Channel 4 Book, Belfast

Hall JW, McClain JL (1991) The Cambridge history of Japan, vol 4, Early Modern Japan. Cambridge University Press, Cambridge

Hall JW, Toyoda T (1977) Japan in the Muromachi age. University of California Press, Berkeley

Haraguchi T (1966) Satsuma domain at the end of the Edo period (Bakumatsu no Satsuma). Chuō Kōronsha, Tokyo

Hayami A (1973) Historical demography of early modern villages (Kinsei Nōson no Rekishi-Jinkōgaku-teki Kenkyū). Tōyō Keizai Shimpōsha, Tokyo

Hayami A (1976) Introduction: the emergence of economic society and its characteristics (Joron: keizaishakai no seiritsu to sonotokushutu). In: Socio-economic History Society (eds) (1977) Searching for new historical view of Edo-era (Atarashii Edo-Jidaishizō wo Motomete). Tōyō Keizai Shimpōsha, Tokyo, pp 3–18

Hayami A (2001) The historical demography of pre-modern Japan. University of Tokyo Press, Tokyo

Hayami A (2009) Population, family and society in pre-modern Japan. Global Oriental, Folkstone

Hayami A (2010) Population and family in early-modern Central Japan. International Research Center for Japanese Studies, Kyoto

Hayami A, Saito O, Toby RP (1999) The economic history of Japan: 1600–1990, vol 1, Emergence of economic society in Japan, 1600–1859. Oxford University Press, Oxford

Hicks JR (1969) A theory of economic history. Oxford University Press, Oxford

Jansen MB (1989) The Cambridge history of Japan, vol 5, The nineteenth century. Cambridge University Press, Cambridge

Kokushō I (1928) A study of peasant uprisings (Hyakushō Ikki no Kenkyū). Iwanami Shoten, Tokyo

Mass JP (1976) The Kamakura Bakufu: a study in documents. Stanford University Press, Stanford

A. Hayami, *Japan's Industrious Revolution*, Studies in Economic History,
DOI 10.1007/978-4-431-55142-3

Mayet M (1893) Impoverishment of the Japanese peasantry and its relief measures (Nihon nōmin no hihei to sono kyūsaisaku), lecture delivered before Prince Arisugawa, translated and published by Daitaro Aoyama, Tokyo
Morris D (1999) Land and society. In: Shively DH, McCullough WH (eds) The Cambridge history of Japan, vol 2, Heian Japan. Cambridge University Press, Cambridge, pp 183–235
Ōishi S (1961) Economic policies of the Kyōhō reforms (Kyōhō Kaikaku no keizai seisaku). Ochanomizu Shobō, Tokyo
Saito O (1976) The interest rate and the supply of money. In: Mataji Umemura et al (eds) Collected papers on the quantitative economic history (Sūryō Keizaishi Ronshū) I. Nihon Keizai Shinbunsha, Tokyo
Sekiyama N (1957) The population of Japan in the early modern period (Kinsei Nihon no jinkō-kōzō). Yoshikawa Kōbunkan, Tokyo
Shimbo H (1978) Commodity prices and economic development in the early modern period (Kinsei no Bukka to Keizai Hatten). Tōyō Keizai Shimpōsha, Tokyo
Shively DH, McCullough WH (1999) The Cambridge history of Japan, vol 2, Heian Japan. Cambridge University Press, Cambridge
Slicher van Bath BH (1963) The agrarian history of Western Europe. Edward Arnold, London
Toby RP (1984) State and diplomacy in early modern Japan: Asia in the development of the Tokugawa Bakufu. Princeton University Press, Princeton
Tonomura H (1992) Community and commerce in late medieval Japan: the corporate villages of Tokuchin-ho. Stanford University Press, Redwood City
Torao T (1961) A study of the "Handen" system (Handen Shūju-hō no Kenkyū). Yoshikawa Kōbunkan, Tokyo
White J (1995) Ikki: social conflict and political protest in early modern Japan. Cornell University Press, New York
Yamamura K (1990) The Cambridge history of Japan, vol 3, Medieval Japan. Cambridge University Press, Cambridge

MIX
Papier aus verantwortungsvollen Quellen
Paper from responsible sources
FSC® C105338

If you have any concerns about our products,
you can contact us on
ProductSafety@springernature.com

In case Publisher is established outside the EU,
the EU authorized representative is:
Springer Nature Customer Service Center GmbH
Europaplatz 3, 69115 Heidelberg, Germany

Printed by Libri Plureos GmbH
in Hamburg, Germany